# I Got Drunk at my
# Baby Shower

# I Got Drunk at my
# Baby Shower
## Our Successful Surrogacy Story

Susan Bowen          Heidi Thompson

TATE PUBLISHING
AND ENTERPRISES, LLC

Published by Tate Publishing & Enterprises, LLC
127 E. Trade Center Terrace | Mustang, Oklahoma 73064 USA
1.888.361.9473 | www.tatepublishing.com

Tate Publishing is committed to excellence in the publishing industry. The company reflects the philosophy established by the founders, based on Psalm 68:11,
*"The Lord gave the word and great was the company of those who published it."*

Book design copyright © 2013 by Tate Publishing, LLC. All rights reserved.
*Cover design by Allen Jomoc*
*Interior design by Caypeeline Casas*

Published in the United States of America

ISBN: 978-1-62746-838-1
1. Biography & Autobiography / Personal Memoirs
2. Family & Relationships / Parenting / Motherhood
13.07.24

# Dedication

*Susan: To Heidi, Payton, Jordan, and my father, Roger, for tapping both Heidi and I on the shoulder to write this book. We listened. We hope you like it. Heidi: JC, AT, and MJC—all my love, always.*

# *Preface*

For years, I thought I would never have children, let alone become the type of mother who looks back on pictures and tears up, yearning for time back at each stage of life with them. I find myself wanting back the chance to hold them one more time as babies; watch them crawl for the first time; react as I read them their favorite books; and discover water in the bath, textures on their tongue, the feeling of wind on their face, and the sight of snow for the first time. As the saying goes, it all goes by so fast! How do you take enough time to enjoy every minute? The truth is, you can't. Life goes on.

Meanwhile, day to day, errands need to be done, the house needs straightening, laundry needs to be put away, we need to go to work, dinner needs to be cooked, and all of life's roadblocks can make you forget what happened in the last twenty-four hours, let alone the previous four-and-a-half years. I'll tell you one thing, though, sometimes on one of those busy "get up and get ready for school" mornings where no one is quite doing what they're supposed to, and not listening, it gets frustrating. Everyone is on edge, but I need to prioritize. If I don't pause with them then, it's always that very night when Payton and Jordan come home from school that I have them sit in my lap to cuddle and watch television. I try to hold onto the precious day with the gifts they are because, my God, they are just *flying* by.

I reflect a lot on the miracle that was given to Jeff and me by our angel Heidi on September 30, 2008. Writing this book has given me the opportunity to recognize and reflect on my unique journey to motherhood. As if I wasn't grateful enough before, I'm blessed now by Heidi's wonderful request to jot the journey down on paper.

My hope is that all who read the book find the humor, love, perseverance, honesty, and joy that I relived while writing my portion of the memoir down. Life is a gift; blessings are bountiful. Never give up on what you want, and even when God and the universe don't answer prayers right away, the answers do come at the right time. There's always a reason why our requests are put on hold. Oh, and laugh...*a lot!*

—Susan

Since the boys were born, the Bowens have kept a YouTube channel to share with friends and family. Two videos that prevalently stick out in my mind included one of Jeff and Susan bringing the boys home to Chicago for the first time and Susan's mom, Sharon, running up to them in the airport, smiling widely. All of a sudden, she stopped, placed her hand over her heart, and looked toward the sky, exclaiming, "Honey, they are here!" What made this so special is that I knew she was talking to Susan's father, Roger, who their family had lost to cancer during our journey.

The second video that really stopped me in my tracks was created in May 2009, when the boys were about eight months old. By that time I had just received a sixty-three-hour prep course to try to obtain a real estate license. I had barely opened the box when I was watching another video of the twins having their first taste of ice cream. Susan's mom was feeding them while Susan was filming. The two boys, round-faced cherubs who bounced and kicked in their chairs hoping for more, lapped it up with zeal. Smiling at them, looking adorable and healthy, I sat back and cherished the sight.

But what happened next I was most assuredly not prepared for. At the end of the video, Susan's mom, Sharon, said, "You tell me when to stop, Mommy."

As random as that seems, it struck me as if someone hit me upside the head. I realized that Sharon was also given an opportunity to have a component of their relationship that they may have never experienced had this journey not taken place. They have now been able to relate not only as mother and daughter, but also as mother to mother. Distinctly, I heard a voice deep inside my head say, "You need to put that course aside, and you need to write a book about this."

I put the sixty-three-hour course aside but dragged my feet on retelling our story. I'm not an avid reader or writer. What I can be is a procrastinator. It was not until years later, while visiting Susan and the boys, that it occurred to me to get serious about this project. While in their basement playroom spending time with

Susan, my husband Rusty and the twins, Susan casually mentioned that she had told her friends that her surrogate was coming for a visit. I know in the depths of my heart what Susan meant, but it once again hit me that others "would never understand." It sounded as mundane as "My accountant is coming for an appointment." (No disrespect meant for that trade, of course!)

*With the simple label of "surrogate," they would never know the depths of emotion that each of us went through together, or what any other couple trying to cope with infertility experience*, I thought. That prompted me to suggest to Susan the idea of us telling each of our sides of this journey. As she's the "anti-procrastinator," this venture shortly began.

Although being a gestational surrogate was never on my bucket list, I am thankful that I was able to be a part of something that's bigger than just my own life. Who knows what footprint these two little lives may leave on this world? Knowing Susan as I do now, these two boys will only add exponential positivity to the world.

During the time I was carrying the twins and relating our story, many people wanted to ask questions but would almost always preface them with "If it's not too much of a personal question, and you don't have to answer if you don't want to, but…" There seemed to be such an innate inquisitiveness about the surrogacy process, but so many people were very hesitant to ask. It was akin to a child wanting to tear the corner of the wrapping on the Christmas presents under the tree but fearing they'd get into trouble, so they would just leave it alone even though they really want to know.

The most important reason for this memoir is to relay our lessons learned throughout our two-and-a-half-year surrogacy process. We all agreed that the long journey and all the diversions were guideposts that sustained us until it was time for the Bowen boys to make their entrance into the world. The whole journey was *their* fate, not so much ours. Looking back now, it becomes clear to understand and accept that sometimes things don't work out to your liking at that desired moment, but making the best of any situation, staying calm, and carrying on could bring you to an even better outcome than you could have ever hoped for!

—Heidi

# Chapter 1

# SUSAN

Ironically enough, children were never a priority to me. I know, I know—odd way to start a surrogacy memoir, but it's the truth. When I married Jeff back in 1998, we were focused on being newlyweds. It was our future, and we couldn't imagine including anyone into it just yet. At our wedding, we received a framed quote that said, "We may not have it all together, but together we have it all." I still think that is one of the greatest sentiments ever. I'm at a different point in life now that has changed tenfold since our first year of marriage, but there is no doubt that having Payton and Jordan today are part of "having it all"—the chance to love and parent two wonderful blessings brought to us in an uncommon way.

Life has a funny way of wandering astray from what you plan. What's that saying, "Make a plan, God laughs"? Anyway, as Jeff and I sat on the couch, snuggling and watching television, we rambled into sentimental discussions about our future and what it might hold. Though we never discounted the idea of children, we never planned on it right away. But in 2001, my gynecologist frowned during my annual examination.

"Susan," she said, "you've had a history of abnormal pap smears, correct?"

"Yeah, some abnormal cells have been found and removed a couple times."

The gynecologist stretched off the rubber gloves until they snapped. She walked to the sink and pumped a few squirts of the high-grade antibacterial soap. "Well," she said thoughtfully as she scrubbed, "we might want to consider a few options."

*Oh boy*, I thought. I listened attentively as she sat back on the stool across from the examination table with the two metal "horse stirrups" attached.

"This gives us cause for concern. After removing the abnormal matter, it still isn't going away. And this time, it's a more aggressive, epithelial form of abnormal cells. It's no longer on the outside of your cervix. It's in the layers of tissue underneath. We might want to consider sterner action."

My eyes widened as she continued to talk. To my horror, she recommended a hysterectomy as a preemptive measure because my tests revealed precancerous tendencies. Later, we learned it was much more severe than I had imagined.

Upon the shocking news, I discussed the possibilities with Jeff. Considering such an intense "end all, be all" procedure is never an easy conversation to have. He crossed his arms as if protecting himself from the truth, staring down at the table. We knew it boiled down to two options: one, get that uterus outta there so I'd have guaranteed safety, or two, leave it in because maybe we would want to try someday anyway, despite the risks. There was a strong possibility that even with an aggressive monitoring schedule, there was a chance an "all clear, try and get pregnant now" plan of action could lead to the cancer coming back even stronger with pregnancy hormones. Of course, there was also a chance it would not. Unfortunately, these plans were mutually exclusive.

"Honey, I can't make the decision for you," said Jeff impassively. "It's your body." Uncomfortable silence. Then, "I just know that I want you to be safe."

Safety first. If I had kids but couldn't guarantee I'd always be there, or would be there unhealthy, what was the point? My family had a nasty history of cancer, and that was also a huge guiding point for me. In my family, it seems you either die of cancer or live to be over ninety, not a lot of in between. The decision became easier from that line of thinking onward. That's when I made the difficult decision of a partial hysterectomy in 2002—that's the one where you keep the hormone makers, the ovaries. I didn't know then that I would come to need them for reasons other than avoiding going into menopause at twenty-nine.

Looking around our relatively new humble abode, the situation was surreal. As I looked at our new oversized family room sofa set, our dining room set handed down from my grandparents, and the wall collages depicting great times from our wedding and get-togethers with friends, I realized how young our life together was. There was that picture of my friends and I yelling "cheers" and smashing together our plastic punch cups at Halloween. We were decked out in multicolored wigs and coated in an inch thick of costume makeup. Each photo showed a couple that was active, fresh-faced, smiling, and young.

Our marriage *was* only three years old; we were a "yuppie" couple traveling together, dining out together, shopping together, and enjoying what life gave us. To remove all possibility of childbearing so early on was a jarring event. But I was petrified. I knew I had to do what I felt was right for me, potentially in order to survive.

*And there goes my oven,* I thought with a rueful smile.

With the passage of time, we soon forgot the whispers of childbearing possibilities. They floated away from our minds as we focused on other things. It wasn't an easy time, but we moved on from that "stuck" feeling and really got ourselves involved in living life, having projects, and buying homes. With laughter and joint enthusiasm, we made phone calls and went to Home Depot, using our hands and ingenuity as catharsis. Jeff and I fixed houses up and sold them until finally, in 2004, we landed in our current home. The question of children was relegated to a remote chamber in my brain. I was savoring life.

And then the forgotten thirty-fourth birthday unexpectedly fell into my lap.

"What happened to my youth?" I cried jokingly as I looked down at my birthday cake. "You know you're old when ya can't even fit enough candles on the surface area of your cake—and this is a big cake!"

With my face in an orange glow, I leaned forward with my hair scooped back in my hand and blew as hard as I could. To the moans of my friends, a stubborn four candles remained.

Though I enjoyed the night and the fact that "calories don't count" on birthdays, something unsettling cemented to the pit of my stomach—and it wasn't the sugary icing. I wouldn't say I felt old, but I knew something from my life prior to that moment was rapidly chugging away like a locomotive into the sunset.

It wasn't long afterward that a friend of mine offered unsolicited advice. "If you ever decide you want kids, maybe I can be the surrogate?"

"Yeah, she has those hips," joked my other friend, after which she was elbowed in the rib.

"But I'm serious," said the former. "Call me up. I loved being pregnant. I'm *good* at it."

"Thanks, guys," I said. "But I don't *foresee* that happening. I wouldn't even know where to begin."

Later, Jeff and I lay in bed. Although I was quick to decline my friend's offer, maybe there was something to this surrogacy idea. I'd be lying if I said that I didn't try to have kids for the sake of completing a family. Somehow, as we aged, I felt more and more guilty about my inability to bear children. We enjoyed life okay, but I just wondered if Jeff felt there was a blatant gap in our lives that needed filling. The guilt putrefied in my heart as time wore on, dragging me down and beginning to weigh on my thoughts. Although we ate at the dinner table in the comfortable silence that accompanied our years together, I couldn't help but overanalyze it.

*What if Jeff is unhappy?*
*What if he's bored with just the two of us?*
*Is this really all it will ever be?*

I glanced down at our dog, Snickers. As he wagged his tail and panted with a hint of a smile on his snout, images of a chubby-cheeked toddler wrapping his short arms around his large, furry neck materialized. I smiled at the thought before sinking back into my guilt as Jeff asked how my day went.

Eventually, the idea of adoption arose. Jeff and I sat in bed, my unread book sitting open on my lap. At my mention of it, Jeff shook his head exaggeratedly on the pillow to the point the headboard started tapping against the wall.

"There's always the possibility someone will want the kids back," he said. "That's drama waiting to happen."

"Well," I began, "there are surrogate parents…"

Eureka! Surrogacy! Jeff and I smiled at each other at the concept of our own biological kids. The fact it was possible was a breath of fresh air into our marriage. Maybe, just maybe, this was something attainable. As Jeff was the only son in his family, images of a young boy to carry on the name stuck to the brain. Even a precious little girl would be a blessing. The offer from my birthday arose for surrogacy. Was that a real possibility?

With a twinkle in my eye, I leaned toward Jeff. "Let's start researching."

It was time to knock on the doors of those who so generously offered. No stone unturned, right? My friend and I were attending one of those tiered marketing parties where the host gets a ton of loot. We stepped away to fill our cocktail glasses (everyone orders more when they have a couple drinks—all of us who have hosted even one candle party know that). What would be a better, more relaxed time to just bring it up? The question came out of my mouth before I had time to stop it.

"So were you serious about potentially carrying a baby for Jeff and I? Can we borrow your oven to put our bun in?"

She almost spurted out her drink; her eyes darted and she gave me a wan smile. "Uh, well—that's a quick decision! I mean, sure."

My friend waved it off, flipping her hair back. "How do we go about it?"

"Well, we're still doing the research. But I do know of a fertility clinic nearby. It's worth investigating."

"I'm in."

We talked in depth about what led me to the decision, what it would be like, and all the nitty-gritty ideas. Or so we thought, anyway. We hugged it out and called it a night.

When I got home that night, I told Jeff the news. Being the eternal realist that he is, he was skeptical but curious enough about idea, so off we went to investigate further. After finding out medically that my friend would be cleared to be a surrogate, Jeff and I went to the fertility clinic to get the first steps. I promptly discussed everything we learned with my friend and all things still seemed a "go." I offered her gym memberships and personal training after the baby was born if she felt out of shape and offered to be there for any and everything she needed. I thought, *This could really work! This could be it!*

One fateful night, we had the couple over to our home, and after dinner, I wanted to express to her husband that I was so honored that she offered and blurted out the laundry list of everything we would "do for them." Well, that was a bit premature. We found out as if an anvil landed on our heads that she hadn't discussed it with her husband yet, this idea of our bun in her oven, and it was obvious he was not on board.

Yikes! What had we done? We understood his perspective and right to have an opinion, but talk about an awkward moment! I wanted to crawl in my fireplace and burst into flames.

Our relationship with them was rocky for a bit but repaired itself as all worthwhile relationships do, even stronger today. You see, as I'll keep repeating through my memoir, everything happens for a reason.

Backtracking to the meeting Jeff and I had with the fertility clinic in this attempt, we were turned off by the head physician there. In hindsight, all things weren't in order there to begin with, but in these endeavors, you sometimes have to jump in, feet first, throw stuff at the wall, and see what sticks. *This* didn't stick. Heavyhearted, we packed up the idea for the moment and took some time to really acknowledge what happened and what we might be in for if we continued down this path. Adoption, not an option and first crack at a surrogacy match, not a fit, I'll admit I wanted to quit. Thankfully, we didn't.

# Chapter 2

# HEIDI

Life sure can be eventful, can't it? Sometimes the best laid plans, well…you know! My plans as a single mother in the year 2000 were always geared toward finding an answer to "How else can I earn the income needed to get by without having to be absent from my children from 7:00 am through 11:00 pm five days a week as I have done for so many years?" I never expected that question to lead me on a path that would introduce me to the concept of becoming a gestational surrogate. Although I consider myself a mother first and foremost, I had to juggle two jobs very frequently in order to support my sons, aged thirteen and ten, and my seven-year-old daughter. Luckily, my parents moved into the apartment building right next door and were the best stand-in parents anyone could ask for. What helped me get through so often was to focus on my blessings. It was an ironic situation though, always looking for ways to earn additional income while trying to gain extra time to spend with my kids. Busting my bottom to make their lives "better," even though their grandmother was there for them, they still lacked their mom.

Weary of struggling to cover it all, I took an inventory of my skills in the year 2000 to see where I could have better prospects.

"Now, what am I good at?" I asked myself, tapping my pen on the table. Smiling in jest, I added, "Well, you did have three pretty good runs with pregnancy—never having one day of morning sickness and always feeling healthier than when *not* pregnant."

As if a higher power jumped into my private conversation, I soon saw a small ad in the classified section of the *Orlando Sentinel* placed by a lawyer from West Palm Beach, Florida, which is about two hundred miles or a three-hour drive away from my home. Interested, I stuck my nose in that page and saw it advertised a need for gestational surrogates.

Although I was facetious while thinking about how easily my body endured three pregnancies, I had never heard of the prospect of being a paid incubator for another family's hopes and dreams. That gave me cause to pause and sincerely be introspective regarding my pregnancies.

*I have to be honest with myself,* I thought. Recalling my first pregnancy in the late '80s, I was a tender nineteen-year-old. I was always responsible but had plenty of growing up to do. As I delivered my first son, reality swept over me with the force of a tidal wave. I was a parent. Striking me more that moment was looking back on the duration of my pregnancy. I didn't have the emotional bond or the instantaneous overjoyed feeling that I assumed I should've had.

Holding that small child, extending its apricot-sized fist toward me, I froze. At that moment, I realized the dependence of this tiny being. I knew I loved him more than life itself, but when I remembered the pregnancy and delivery, I was torn up.

*Am I a monster? Am I really someone who's cold and unfeeling? Why don't I automatically feel completely bonded to this beautiful baby boy?*

With the lack of research on mental health issues compared to what's out there today, along with the general attitudes back then, I realized that there was no way that I could vocalize my apparent lack of feelings to anyone. I cannot stress enough how much I love all three of my children, and it did not take long for me to form a loving bond—within days—but it is a fact. I did *grow* to love my children to the extent I now do today, but it was hard swallowing my initial feelings.

Having acknowledged to myself that I had thrice experienced pregnancy while not feeling the emotional attachment immediately, I knew I could be a viable candidate for a gestational surrogacy, should that opportunity ever present itself to me. With that introspection, I called the phone number listed and left a voicemail that I was interested in additional information. After days turned into weeks without a response, I didn't give much thought to the prospect, pursuing many other work opportunities. Most turned out to be dead ends until the opportunity to become a flight attendant arose in 2001.

"Thank God," I said with a sigh of relief. "A decent income, a flexible schedule, more time with the kids, and even an opportunity to travel with them."

Five years passed. No, I didn't have a forty-hour per week office job, but financial circumstances never evolved to permit as much time with the kids as quickly as I'd preferred.

When my kids were saddened by my departures, it tore my heart out every time. If they ever vocalized their not wanting me to leave, I consoled them with, "Maybe next year I won't have to fly as much and can be home more with you." It was my mantra; I repeated it so often I hoped it would be true. However, what hurt more than their own hurt was their indifference, their acceptance that Mom just wouldn't be around. Something had to change.

In 2005, my eldest son had started his senior year of high school. As he bolted out of the door to zoom off to class one last time, I crossed my arms and leaned against the doorway. A montage floated through my head, showing a reel of our years together and surfacing regrets for frequently proposing ideas of spending one-on-one time with him, yet never making the time to follow through. Averaging being home only about ten-to-twelve days out of a month, I knew I wasn't the nurturing presence I strove to be. Communicating through cell phones and the Internet helped make the situation bearable, of course, but it wasn't the same.

Speaking with my new husband, Rusty, during a sacred moment of alone time, I ran my fingers through my hair. "I just feel so bad—I'll never get these years back with them."

Rusty leaned forward with his arms on his knees, seated in the easy chair in the corner of the living room as he paused in thought. Having never been married before or had any other children, he was as concerned as I was. "What had you considered in the past? Maybe we could revisit one of those options."

The article back in 2000 popped into my mind like a flickering neon sign. "Well, there was becoming a gestational surrogate…" I winced in anticipation of his response, but he looked genuinely interested.

"Yeah? You always said pregnancy was easy for you."

Smiling in gratitude, I was relieved. Rusty is a very conservative, extremely patriotic family man, so even though we talked about my interest into looking into becoming a surrogate when I was a single mom, I was not sure of his stance on the subject. Unfortunately, because we were house hunting as our lease was up on our rental, the idea was filed away for the time being.

That is, until I took my daughter to the pediatrician in May of 2006. Browsing a family magazine as we sat in the waiting room, I was taken aback at the huge color ad on the page I opened to. Leaning forward and reading it, I couldn't believe my eyes. Even my daughter Cayla glanced over at me, wondering why I was so rigid.

"Egg donation and surrogacy agency? This is ten minutes from our house!" I muttered. How astonishing it was to see the concept had evolved from an obscure blurb in the legal section of the classifieds, treating the process as somewhat of an underground procedure, to a mainstream, full-page advertisement in a family magazine!

When the nurse called our names, I quickly approached the desk. "Do you mind if I take this with me? There's something of extreme importance to me in here."

Surprisingly they were okay with it, and I held it close to my chest as my daughter was weighed and had her temperature taken.

That night, I put it on the coffee table in front of Rusty, tapping the ad with my finger—as if he needed guidance to find the colorful ad! After he glanced at it, our eyes met without a word. With raised eyebrows, we shrugged and all but stated, "It doesn't hurt to try."

Our adventure awaited us. We researched the agency through our local chapter of the Better Business Bureau and any other means we could find. Feeling comfortable that they were reputable, we filled out preliminary information and requested an application that same day.

Prior to throwing ourselves into this wholeheartedly, I called a meeting in the den with my children. They squeezed together like sardines on the love seat, their faces impassive.

"Here's what's going on," I began, "and I won't do this without your blessing." After my explanation, I waited for their responses. Even though my goal was to gain time at home with my children, if they did not want this experience brought into their lives, then I would have dropped the notion promptly.

Our kids had typical responses for their genders and age. The boys, being in their late teens, merely said, "I guess so." That translated to "If it doesn't affect my life, then I guess it's okay."

"How can I tell you that I'll be okay with something if I've never been through it before?" piped up my daughter on the couch.

Rusty and I exchanged glances. *Pretty astute for a thirteen-year-old*, I thought. Knowing they were open-minded to the idea, I dove in enthusiastically.

Days later, the hard copy of the application came in the mail, and it was quickly filled out and returned along with requested family photos. There were questions about my physical attributes, medical history, prior pregnancies (because it is a customary initial qualification to have had at least one successful pregnancy), preferences of race and sexual orientation for matching purposes, and also essay questions such as what my goals were in assisting an intended family by being their birth mother.

During June 2006, I received a phone call from an assistant at the agency shortly after submitting the application and was given an appointment time to call in and have a preliminary phone interview with the owner of the agency. Once again it was like a kismet event because the interview was arranged on the day that my eldest son would be busy with his daylong college orientation. We had nothing planned but to wait for him while lounging on a local beach.

"I'm waiting to get pregnant again while 'my baby' is heading off to college," I told Rusty as we walked along the sand, waves gently rolling underfoot. "It's all very strange but exciting."

Rusty linked his hand with mine, and we looked ahead at the palm-tree dotted path of our stroll. I grinned at him. The sun shone a little brighter down the coast.

# Chapter 3

# SUSAN

Jeff and I were now business partners. Our business? Finding a doctor and a fertility clinic with a better fit. Oh, and one other tiny detail, a surrogate. We had the ingredients, but we still needed an oven. Thankfully we had some friends who were struggling with something similar on their own fertility journey, but they were putting their bun back in their own oven.

"There's this one in the city with many monitoring locations. You would just love the doctor and the center—*so* professional and friendly," she said, sitting closely beside her husband who nodded on cue. "I can write the name down and everything. Check it out!"

"Sounds like it's worth a shot," I said.

With that, we embarked to the fertility center to check out our chances. Jeff and I didn't say much, knowing that everything relied on the outcome of this meeting. Despite only being thirty-four, I crossed my fingers that my eggs were still in good shape—that this could be a real possibility for us. Holding my breath, I could only breathe deeply again when I knew the results.

When the nurse called us back, we already felt taken care of just seeing her genuine smile. The doctor was even better; he asked us about what we did professionally, we commiserated about the weather, and he demonstrated that he was one of the most patient, good listeners I had seen in a doctor. Already, this felt like a better fit than the first fertility clinic.

Toward the end of the evaluation, the doctor leaned forward on the stool and laced his fingers together. "Judging by your age and how healthy you are, you'll likely experience success," he assured us.

Jeff and I grinned like kids on Christmas. Good news already!

"Now we just need to find an agency or something," I said. "One item crossed off the list, ten more to go."

The doctor looked thoughtful. "Well, I do know someone…she was one of my former patients. She owns her own company that matches egg donors and surrogates with intended parents."

"Awesome!" I exclaimed. "Is it near here?"

"It's in Illinois, yeah. As far I know, they can match you up with anybody nationwide. That increases your odds of finding someone sooner."

The more he talked, the more excited we became, nodding faster and faster as our grins spread wider on our faces. He said as long as we maintained a way for both parties to be monitored through the process, and that the surrogate could travel to Chicago for embryo transfers, we could find a surrogate from anywhere.

The next step in the fertility center process was to have a psyche evaluation. After we "passed" that, we would be on the road to parenthood…or so we hoped. Again, it was interesting during the psyche evaluation how "businesslike" Jeff and I had become about the prospect. In hindsight, it was a protection mechanism, a window into our relationship. It proved how successful we were and remain when life revolves around a common goal or project. We were one staunch force to be reckoned with during each step of the way.

We were lucky we hadn't told anyone of our first attempt to use a surrogate. To date, we hadn't had to erase any expectations. Because of this, we knew instinctively *not* to let anyone in on the new journey yet either—not until we had a few more ducks in a row, or at least in the pond. We knew we'd have support the moment we needed it from our dear friends and family, so why make them wait and hope for something that may never happen? It was bad enough that we had to.

I knew then and there that any further attempts would be kept secret until everything was certain.

After we passed our evaluation, we promptly made a call to the consultant that was referred to us and scheduled a meeting with her shortly before Thanksgiving of 2006.

"The butterflies in my stomach are violent," I told Jeff. "I feel like I'm gonna barf."

The day we met the consultant, she chose to meet us in a public library. The room she ushered us into was entirely enclosed in glass; I could see my peeking face reflected back in it.

The three of us greeted each other and shared an awkward smile. I saw all the activity outside beyond the walls. Somehow I felt like I was in a bubble for everyone to see, especially since the reflections made about four duplicates. It made me look more clearly into myself, wondering if this was it—if we were *really* about to begin the journey to parenthood!

As she opened her mouth to discuss the company and its services, the hope continued to bubble in my chest like a newly opened bottle of champagne. It sounded so promising! I tried not to get ahead of myself and imagine holding my own cooing mini-me bundled in blankets. I think Jeff and I were still not convinced that there were angels out there who would gladly offer to be an incubator for us. The curiosity and potential alone made writing the check a no-brainer.

Walking silently to the car, I felt not only excited but also exhilarated. We had just jumped off of a cliff and wondered if there would be any way we'd land on our feet.

"Jeff," I said on the ride home, "I think I'm getting ahead of myself with this excitement. I want to make sure we draw our lines in the sand, if you will."

"Right," he said. "Let's maintain logic. We want to make sure we continue to make decisions carefully and with a lot of consideration. And people may think we are crazy."

"I know, I thought of that and remember hearing stories about other people and what they would try in order to complete their families. We have both shaken our heads at some of those stories…but now it's going to be us. My brain is going a thousand miles an hour." I groaned.

Honestly, it only took a few hours to reset my mode of thinking and erect a giant brick wall in my mind. It would halt me if I thought too far in advance or let my emotion dictate action.

*Just wait until the agency gets back to us,* I told myself.

Though I expected a couple of weeks for them to get back to me, it only took twenty-four hours.

"Hey, Susan! We have three candidate profile matches for you."

"*Already?*" I asked in disbelief.

Before I knew it, I was motioning for Jeff to get on the computer so we could check them out. That was it! There were real, flesh-and-blood surrogate candidates who would be our angels in providing the ultimate sacrifice of incubating *our* flesh and blood. The onslaught of flurried emotions was so disparate—excited, skeptical, and overwhelmed all at once!

The first profile we looked at belonged to a Heidi Thompson.

"Oh my God, she's real and she actually wants to have our baby," I said, breathing heavily and trying to calm down. At this point, we didn't have pictures of the candidates, just their profiles, but our overall feeling from Heidi's was just comfort and warmth. It oozed from the pages. Something about her character was honest and reached out to me. We lingered on her before we continued on to the rest.

Within two days, we had seven more profiles to peruse. Each profile we looked at was so different from the next, yet all were willing to give their body up for the sake of incubating human life for another family.

*Simply breathtaking,* I thought. However, we kept coming back to the first, Heidi. She gave such heartfelt answers about wanting to be a vessel in someone else's miracle.

"They're in Florida," said Jeff. "But we can still use them?"

"If they agree to come up for embryo transfers. But here it says they're open to working with people out of state." Somehow I was touched. They were making themselves available wherever needed.

That's when we picked up the phone and dialed our consultant. "We need to make sure she's available," I murmured to Jeff. This whole experience showed us how delicate and time-sensitive the procedure was. We could call and find out she was already serving as some-one else's surrogate. There were a select few options, truly revealing to us how unique the situation was and how priceless it would be once we succeeded. It would be worth every penny and more.

We held our breath as we waited to hear about the status of Heidi.

"Oh, Heidi," said the consultant, seeming to know everyone from the top of her head. "Yes, she's available."

Jeff and I had a subtle party as we jumped up and down and silently screamed while the consultant sat on speakerphone. "Oh, that's great! Do you think we could set up an appointment with her and Rusty then?"

The consultant gave us her contact information and said she would give Heidi a heads-up. I couldn't believe it. My vision of our little one was slowly materializ-ing into a reality. Even though Jeff and I talked about everything like it was real, it didn't sink into mind yet. Whenever we talked about it, our eyes widened and our shoulders snuck up toward our ears in rigidity. We were still struggling with disbelief.

In spite of that, we made plans in mid-December of 2006 to have a conference call with Heidi over our lunch break. Jeff and I got ready for work that morning in deafening silence. Neither of us had words to express what the call might lead to.

"Well, I'll see you at twelve fifteen," Jeff said, standing at the doorway as he shimmied his jacket on.

"Wow…yeah, twelve fifteen. Yes. I'll see you then."

That day, the minutes dribbled by like tree sap. My eyes kept glancing to the clock and waiting until we'd hear from this saintly woman. Although we had exchanged a few e-mails, it was going to be surreal to speak with her—to confirm she was a real person who was on a mission to potentially help us, not a person we had mentally constructed in wishful thinking. My nerves wouldn't calm.

I left my office at eleven thirty to drive to Jeff's office to meet him. I don't even remember the drive; I just landed at his conference table somehow. We closed the door and made the call into the conference line.

"Hello?" we said on our end. The agency owner from the agency Heidi "came" from answered back with a friendly hello and made the introductions.

"Hello, Susan?" Heidi had a sweet, meek voice. I'd soon discover she had a personality to match.

"Heidi!" I said breathlessly. There she was!

Soon Rusty and Jeff joined in the conversation. We all recited "Nice to meet yous" before awkwardly falling silent. It was a blind date as we all sought to find the perfect match. We generally stuck to the introductory questions as we tried to get to know one another. In spite of all the pressure lingering overhead, the conversation managed to flow naturally. Immediately I could tell how Rusty and Heidi worked together. She was the quieter, more observant one while Rusty's friendly, booming voice took over.

After the conversation, Jeff stretched out in the chair and asked, "So whaddya think?"

I paused. Not because I was unsure, but because there were so many positive emotions coursing through me. Without knowing this couple intimately, we clicked and it felt right, like we still knew each other prior to that. Sometimes, even without substantial proof, we know without a shadow of a doubt what is right.

Heidi and Rusty's picture—two glowing faces leaning toward each other—constantly waited on the sidelines of my mind. They were a tough act to follow.

# Chapter 4

# HEIDI

When I think about how precarious the surrogate situation was, it's jarring.

I called for my phone interview with the owner of the agency from that serene South Florida beach location.

"Heidi, hey. Would you mind if we considered rescheduling? There are unexpected events, and right now is just not a good time," she said in an urgent tone.

"Um, sure." I was taken aback, even feeling somewhat letdown after having our family onboard for the new experience.

*If it's meant to be, it will get resolved and rescheduled,* I told myself.

Weeks passed. The rescheduled call never occurred. After calling again around the beginning of July 2006 to verify that I was still a surrogate candidate and never getting a response, I put the notion on the backburner. My three teenagers certainly filled my spare time. I just attributed the turn of events to mean it was not meant to work out for us to be surrogate parents and left it at that. With my son's transition into college and purchasing a new house on the horizon, my hands were tied. I would look for other agencies and restart the process later on.

Life always tossed curveballs and distractions. We purchased our house in October of 2006, and we renovated the home for thirty days straight before moving in the beginning of November, right as my husband was having a major operation. His third through sixth vertebrae was to be fused with pins and rods. With so much happening, I made a mental note to check back into the surrogacy prospect after the holiday season.

It's funny that when I stopped actively looking toward making my hope a reality, everything fell into place. Around the beginning of December 2006, right as I settled myself in the computer chair to conduct research on other fertility agencies, my phone rang. Puzzled, I stood up and reached for it over by the futon.

"Hello?"

The woman from the agency, whom I had waited for six months to speak with, finally returned my call!

"I apologize for the delay, but are you still interested in becoming a surrogate with us?"

"Well…yes!" I said. A smile started forming at the corners of my mouth. Six months later, and just out of the blue, this call comes to me? Crazy timing. "Sure! What are the next steps?"

"We'd love it if you could come and have a face-to-face interview with the owner. After that, we'll give you a referral to an ob-gyn that works closely with us."

As she discussed everything on the phone, I felt relieved that I was back on board the baby train without starting back at square one.

From there, I drove to the agency. It was located in an affluent section of town, not some "fly-by-night office in a shady strip mall," as Rusty once joked. I walked up to the office, which was more reminiscent of a Tuscan villa than an agency, and pulled open the double doors. As I glanced around the office, it looked like an exuberantly professional office with high ceilings. My heels reverberated around the lobby as I met with the owner, who was chatty as we had a "meet and greet" session while also providing us insight for the next steps of the process. As soon as I got home, I set up an appointment to proceed with my medical evaluation, which would clear me and document my qualifications in the initial step of becoming a gestational surrogate.

Within a few weeks, we were contacted once again by the agency saying that if we were interested, they had a couple who had viewed our profile on the agency's website and were interested in interviewing us in a teleconference. Of course we were interested in continuing to explore the opportunity.

That would lead to our initial meeting with Susan and Jeff.

Rusty and I sat at the dining room table as we waited for the agency to facilitate the call. He gave my hand a squeeze before we were carried through.

When I first heard Susan, I could tell she was taking the reins. She spoke confidently and pleasantly. I instantly envisioned a successful brunette—though I'd find out the hair color was the only characteristic I was wrong about! She and Jeff didn't hesitate to dive into the personal questions.

"So let's discuss the logistics if you were to be our taxi," Susan said as she began to affectionately dub me.

It was somewhat odd to be sitting in the comfort of our own homes and discussing each intimate detail of our lives to strangers. I perfectly understood why, being a parent myself, and sympathized with their concerns in bringing the new joy into their lives.

Susan progressed through a series of questions as if she had bulleted them on a document in front of her. Jeff stayed more in the background as well while Rusty and Susan were the more boisterous ones. It didn't take long, and they were off on tangents of family life even though the important issues were covered, such as how we'd feel about abstaining for such a long time and so on. Both Susan and Rusty kept the tone from getting too heavy with stories of inside family jokes or practical jokes they enjoyed being a part of, which seem to be at the heart of most families. Letting each other in on such private details of each of our family lives seemed to help form a bond between the four of us that is hard to explain to this day.

As Rusty charmed them with his convivial personality, I paused to feel the reality of inching closer to doing something I never seriously planned on checking off my bucket list, yet I also started to comprehend relational issues in a new light that I never expected. The dynamics of the four of us were unlike anything I'd ever experienced (and assumed that neither had many other people). It was interesting new territory.

"Susan and Jeff have informed us that they wish to move forward with you in their surrogacy. How would *you* feel about moving forward?" said the owner of the surrogacy agency.

Wow, we must have done something right. Although we were made aware that we had been chosen over younger couples, I didn't think, "Cool! We won!" Instead, I asked myself, "What tipped the scale?" especially since it seems more widely accepted that someone younger than thirty-nine years old would have better physical prospects with carrying out a pregnancy.

Rusty was excited for me, having never experienced pregnancy up close and personal before. With his smiles further cementing my resolve, I stopped questioning and accepted the fact this was our future. I guess this item was being added to and crossed off my bucket list.

Spending a great majority of my younger life working as a single parent, I relied on my parents for rearing my children. Although Rusty and I were present figures in their lives, my children's second set of parents was their grandparents. I spoke with my mother every few days and felt more than comfortable bringing up my news.

So sitting cross-legged on the couch and playfully winding my finger around the telephone cord, I called them. After the usual life updates, I announced I had some news.

"Well, you know about how money is tight, and I'm wanting to spend more time with the kids," I began. Mom knew about my struggles since they began.

"Right, go on," she said. Dad was silent and expectant beside her.

"I'm going to be a surrogate for a family in Illinois! They've chosen Rusty and me to carry their child," I explained.

Then there was a tense silence I didn't expect. Biting my lip, I continued explaining, hoping to better inform them—talking about the agency, our consultant, the first phone call with Susan and Jeff, even going toward the compassionate angle after I wasn't hearing any response and bringing up how Susan is a cancer survivor…well, the uncomfortable silence continued to permeate our connection.

Prior to this conversation, I had never discussed my intentions to my parents—not even six years ago when I looked into it for the first time. I didn't know the certainty of it and decided to wait until something substantial occurred. Although we had never discussed the subject, my mother must have heard of the procedure and formed her own opinion because she was strongly against such an event, using terms in our conversation as "black market babies," and "there are so many other children waiting to be adopted, why would you be a part of something that would allow them to be neglected?"

Likewise, my father could not wrap his head around the fact that the baby we would deliver would not have any lineage to our family and could not understand how I could give up "my child," no matter how many times it was explained to him that I would be nothing more than the "taxi."

"The child is not biologically mine, but I'm helping two people experience the joy of parenting that they might not otherwise experience," I persisted, trying to make everything clear. In spite of my deepest wish to help them understand, a rift cracked open between us. They had their established positions on the matter. Taken aback, I felt agitated, complex feelings surface. When I thought about Susan and Jeff's energy and gratitude, I knew there was no way I would back out. I had to live my life for myself, and I knew it was the right avenue to pursue.

As I hung up the phone and saw Rusty enter from the bedroom, I looked up at him with glistening eyes. Without asking, he came to my side and held me close. I pondered this unique situation. Just as if I were carrying on our lineage with a fourth child, there was a lot at stake, a lot of people heavily invested in my pregnancy (whether my child or not—and no matter what people's opinions were on what was rightfully "mine"). It was a situation that doesn't immediately come to mind.

Even though my parents were disappointed and didn't speak to me for two months, I didn't turn back.

"I feel like I'm making my first intentional 'grown-up' decision," I said with a wan smile as Rusty and I talked over breakfast one Sunday morning. "And it happened as I approach age forty."

Rusty staunchly sat at my side. Although my heart was heavy with the hole of my parents' presence in my life, I would honor the path I felt was right.

My mom came to a point a few months afterward where she reached out to me saying that although she and my father could not give their blessing, she hoped we could agree to disagree and restore our relationship, which, thankfully, we have.

❖

All of a sudden, the long wait without any communication from the agency turned into what felt like an onslaught of phone calls and appointments to keep. Soon after, we were to arrange a psychological evaluation.

"So whatever they ask us…"

"We will answer openly and honestly," finished Rusty. That was the motto on our outlook for the evaluation.

"If for some reason they deem us to be crazy, well, we'll have a clear conscience." I laughed.

Our evaluation was held in Orlando. We stepped into a clinic that looked more "homey" than anything, perhaps to put patients at ease. There was a fireplace with a vase with red tulips inside, and a colorful rug with geometrical patterns under our feet. When the psychologist led us into her office, Rusty and I sat on the couch opposite her desk and awaited the questions.

It was basic and stress-free; she went through a list of prepared questions before turning to us and asking questions on the fly:

"So why do you want to be a surrogate family?"

"What are you hoping to gain from the experience?"

"What are your fears in regards to the experience?"

The evaluation took a more conversational turn as we excitedly spoke about the mission we had. The counselor nodded her head and gave neutral responses, leading us to wonder what she thought about us.

One moment that vibrantly sticks out in our memories is when she asked, "How do you handle stress—?"

In unison, Rusty and I enthusiastically blurted out, "We eat!" before she could even finish the question. We looked at each other, and our serious faces cracked into goofy smiles and outright laughter.

Before the evaluation was completed, I was asked to sit in a room by myself and answer a preprinted packet of questions that was approximately five hundred questions long. When I handed it to the receptionist, she simply smiled and said, "Okay, thanks for coming in!"

As Rusty and I walked outside, Rusty said, "That felt odd."

Granted, we did the best we could to answer everything honestly. No guilt there. "It was just weird to feel like we were put under a microscope then given what could be a fake smile and sent on our way," I replied.

"I wonder what she thought of us."

"Whatever it was, we probably have the same diagnosis." We laughed again at the stress question.

Everything must have gone well because the surrogacy agency called us back and said we were cleared.

The more I talked to Jeff and Susan, the more I realized the role I was fulfilling. I was becoming a party to giving the eventual child a set of parents, not only incubating the parent's child. I took on a new perspective while listening to Susan and Jeff and their idea of being parents rather than just looking to get their approval of me. My role was materializing; I was becoming an advocate for the baby.

The negotiations took a few weeks to progress. All the while Susan and Jeff were making determinations on their end regarding health insurance coverage and conferring with friends who work in the legal field in Illinois and Florida, both of our home states. The agency contacted me, asking what I would like to be included for extenuating circumstances in our contract. Reimbursement for events such as selective reduction or other procedures that raise ethical questions had to be addressed.

*Wow,* I thought. Taking a deeper look at my position, I started realizing that if I was in this solely for the added cash flow to our family, the journey would be more risky than one could potentially handle. There were a lot of emotional considerations that seem easy to make until you're landed in that situation, such as "How do I honestly feel this couple would cope with and welcome this child if this baby is born with a birth defect?" It was getting real. I decided I was not moving forward just for monetary gain and started to become very emotionally invested and excited.

We were able to negotiate our contract on a mutually beneficial level. Every imaginable situation was covered, even up to the point where it was addressed that if there were any event that left me expired, but the baby's life would be viable, Rusty agreed to keep me on life support until the baby's birth. The contract covered the possibility of who would receive custody of the child should anything happen simultaneously to Jeff and Susan or in the event of a divorce. Also covered were ethical considerations such as how many eggs were okayed to be transferred during the in-vitro process.

"Wow, it's crazy looking at all this and realizing we're doing this for a family we've never actually met!" I said, running my fingers through my hair. It's easy to forget about the paperwork and the process prior to the pregnancy itself. Many people just imagine a woman receiving the eggs and becoming pregnant right away without consideration for the "what ifs." Myself included. It was a learning experience for everyone. We could only hope that after that point, it would be smooth-sailing.

# Chapter 5

# SUSAN

As we entered 2007, the real adventure began. We got all of our finances in order, verified insurance coverage—what and who would be covered, and if it wasn't, how would we pay for it? There wasn't just medical insurance to think about; we had to purchase and maintain a life insurance policy for Heidi in addition to having a living will for her created through a family lawyer's office. We brought the escrow money to the agency representing Heidi, found attorneys to draw up the paperwork, and started the long uphill climb to parenthood.

By the end of January, we decided it was time to start telling people that we were going to try to start a family (and how we settled on achieving that goal). Scheduling a time for everyone in my family to meet at one of our favorite restaurants, I was uncertain as to how they'd react. I sat in the master bathroom and took longer than usual to get ready, carefully applying mascara and lipstick while I dwelled on the possibility of their reactions. A clock was ticking in my brain, counting down the moments until the news.

"It's such an unusual thing," I told Jeff. "I don't see it happen enough to know what they'll think."

"All we can do is tell them," he said. "We'll deal with the rest after. You know they are going to be thrilled!"

That night, we were a rowdy bunch at a long dining table, exchanging stories about our week with a constant chatter that was interspersed with the characteristic Place family (my maiden name) laughter. Somehow I managed to make small talk and choke down my angel hair marinara with meatballs the size of my head as the pesky questions refused to leave my mind for even a moment.

*How do I bring it up?*

*Where do I start?*

With my heart in my throat, I got the sense that the evening's festivities were dwindling. Carefully setting my fork down on my cleaned plate, I took Jeff's hand in mine. He gave it a squeeze.

*Time to let the bomb drop.*

"Hey, everyone! Jeff and I have an announcement to make."

A few people continued to chatter, so my dad leaned in closer and got the rest of the gang to do the same.

My chest rose as I inhaled. After the corresponding exhale, the news was out. Chins fell to the table. My mom and sister started crying. My brother-in-law sat stunned but smiling, and my dad just looked at me in awe.

I blinked and saw the flurry of emotions at the table. It was still surreal to me, so I felt the need to repeat the information.

"We have decided to use a surrogate to try and have children and have found one. Her name is Heidi, and she and her husband live near Orlando." The words hung in the air. Our server didn't know what to think, looking at our varying degrees of hysterics at the table. My mom motioned for him to come over and shared the news.

By the end of the evening, we went through all the details with them, what we knew of the process to date, and ordered another drink to bask in the moment. As our glasses clinked together during the toast, I reminded myself there was a lot more to come. We all knew that. Still, it was liberating to have it out on the table.

Back then I was quite the scrapbooker: homes, the dog, vacations, you name it. One of my best friends and I were about to embark on a scrapbooking weekend and kicked it off with sushi and sake. Now that I "came clean" with my parents, I wanted to tell the other people nearest and dearest to me.

She was talking about something—I must confess I had no idea what because I was carefully calculating the opportune moment for my news. As I eyed the fish tank in the corner, full of what could've been the newcomers' dinner, I knocked back some sake. When my friend turned to me for input, all I could do was blurt out, "We found a surrogate! Jeff and I are going to be parents!"

Again there was that moment of disbelief. All I could hear was the clanging of chopsticks against the plates and servers' tumbling ice water into patrons' cups. Disbelief, acceptance, then tears of joy swept over

my friend's face. Her eyes turned red as she motioned a
server to come over.

"Two more rounds of sake," she said with a
cracked voice.

The server nodded, seeming to think that the poor,
crying woman could really use it!

From there, I told her the whole story. We paid our
bill, stopped for a bottle of wine, and scrapbooked all
night long, giggling to ourselves about what was to
come. I hadn't wanted anyone else on the retreat to
know, so when we walked back to the hotel, she was
stopping every fifteen minutes saying, "Oh my God!"
Just stopping in her tracks in the middle of the pavement. I laughed and linked my arm with hers to pull
her forward.

"You want something to 'oh my God' about?" I
asked. I had already begun taking hormones and shots
to ready my eggs to harvest, so I told her to come to the
back room with me so I could dose myself at the right
time. Not the usual preparation in the "what to expect"
books!

After plentiful correspondence with Heidi about legal-
ities and logistics, the day came to meet her in the flesh
in June 2007. We e-mailed about meeting together in
the city for Mexican food. I had no idea how I would
eat—it was the meeting of my lifetime!

As Jeff drove us in the car, I couldn't sit still.

"I'm going to hug her so hard I'll break her," I told
him. "But what if she's not the hugging type? Oh, to

hell with it! I'm hugging her until it's borderline inappropriate! She likes Mexican food, right? I forgot. Oh, crap. I hope she doesn't mind where we're meeting. What if she and Rusty get lost?"

I went on and on, chattering Jeff's ear off. As we accelerated after each stoplight, my stomach rose to my throat. Suppressing the squeals within me, I reminded myself to stay levelheaded as we agreed.

Someone else's legs must have carried me to the restaurant. I was in a daze as we approached the lit-up patio, shrouded in shrubberies but guiding us with its upbeat mariachi music. As soon as we opened the door, our heads darted left, right, straight ahead, behind us, and diagonal. We knew what they looked like, but we had to find them during the busy dinner hour. During the crescendo of the music, we saw Rusty. He was a giveaway with his eye patch. There, beside him, was our sacred vessel.

# Chapter 6

# *HEIDI*

There we were in the windy city on the first day of June 2007, getting ready to meet Susan and Jeff for the first time in the flesh. Rusty and I made it to the airport and took a train into the city. We walked to the hotel and up to the desk to check in. Spirits were high until the clerk asked how I'd like to pay for the reservation. Strange, because I had picked up a packet of info from the surrogacy agency back home prior to coming up for our special dinner date with Jeff and Susan. I started flipping through the papers and extracted the sheet that had our confirmation listed.

"There is a reservation," said the clerk, "but it is not completed, and there is not a credit card on file for the charges." Dumbfounded and unsure how this should be processed, I asked if they would be able to call the agency in Florida to square it away. The front desk clerk made the phone call but returned shaking her head.

"There isn't anyone in the office who would be able to access the company credit card."

*Oh my goodness*! Luckily for us, we had room on our own credit card and figured I'd just get reimbursed later. My thoughts immediately went to the fact that I have lived on both sides of that fence, and what if I was in a position that wouldn't allow me to cover the expense? I felt very lucky to be in a place to not have to go there, but the situation did position this agency in a different light for me once again. Everything seemed to have been going smoothly since that six-month lag in communication, so I thought, *I'll just file that away, give them the benefit of the doubt one more time and focus on what's coming up in a few hours, meeting Susan and Jeff in person!*

Rusty and I chose to walk from the hotel to the restaurant, which was about a half-mile away in the misting rain. We finally approached the Mexican restaurant Susan suggested. As we glanced around, we realized we were the first of the bunch of us there and decided to grab a table before it filled up. The place had an inviting "fiesta" atmosphere; normally we're loyal homebodies, but we were excited to be out in Chicago, which really is a great city.

My heart was fluttering, but it was a pleasant kind of nervous. Susan and Jeff were always so kind and likable over the phone, and it would be satisfying to have faces to match their names.

As collected as I was, that changed when I saw Susan and Jeff prance toward us. Susan's arms were outstretched, and she was squealing.

"Oh my God! It's you!" She immediately took me in a tight embrace, like I was a long, lost family member. I worried my heart was beating so fast she could feel it strumming against hers! As she backed away, her smile sliced her face in half, and pure jubilation twinkled in her green eyes. The cut of her smooth blond hair framed her face in a stylish yet professional look. Meanwhile, Jeff and Rusty shook hands heartily.

"Wow, we have so much to talk about," said Susan. "I hope I don't chatter away in my excitement and blow it!"

I laughed. I'm sure we could all feel the frenetic energy trembling and radiating around our table, but it was comforting knowing it was mutual.

"Well, everything looks good. I wonder which I should get," I said, flipping through the menu.

Jeff and Susan exchanged glances. "Look out for Susan," he said. "She'll tell you her top ten favorites here. She's had it all."

"I'm a bit of a Mexican connoisseur," she said with a smile.

Aside from my nervous chatter, the night went well. We continued to get to know one another and discuss the whole process. We all were excited to see what would come of the following day as I was scheduled to have the initial medical examination at their fertility clinic. Somehow, my heart warmed when Susan and Jeff told us the unisex name they had picked out.

"Wow," said Susan, resting her elbows on the table after dinner was done. "I don't know how you manage to do all this, work as a flight attendant and mother your three kids! I guess I have the easy part. Then again, I guess we will both be experts at giving ourselves shots by the end of this."

I found myself opening up more and more to her. Even though we were comparable to a sister-like loyalty, an intimacy derived from embarking on one of life's most rewarding acts together.

Although I had felt adequately prepared knowing that I would be required to take some medication to assist with the procedure, I was unprepared for what I learned the following day. As we were ending our visit in the fertility clinic, Rusty and I were brought into the reproductive endocrinologist assistant's office and given literature that required our signatures. I also received my medication protocol for the month and a half leading up to our first scheduled in-vitro transfer. I was presented with this spreadsheet that was a stinkin' page and a half long! It was like a matrix! As impossible as it sounds I heard a litany of voices in my head saying, "*What?*" "Huh?" "How in the World?" and "Oh my goodness!"—all at the same time!

*I can barely remember to take ten days' worth of antibiotics*, I thought. Now I fully understood Susan's comment from dinner! Then I noticed that the first line required me to start a brand new package on day one— that exact same day—with one birth control pill.

"What are you laughing about?" asked Rusty with a smirk.

"I haven't been on the pill for fourteen years," I said. Since having my tubes tied once my daughter was born in 1993, I wondered how my doctor would prescribe that to me and how I would obtain the pills with the day half over—we still had to make our way back to Orlando! The visit was eye-opening. During my initial agency consultation back in Florida, we had discussed that I would be required to take medication, but it was never addressed in any sort of detail, especially not verifying that I had access to start the protocol with the birth control pill that same day. I was dumbfounded. As I studied the sheet further, I learned that there would be a full month and a half of continual manipulation of my reproductive system with pills, shots, patches, and other methods of medications to prepare for the transfer.

*Wow.* My head spun when we left the office. A marquee of the word "wow" circulated throughout my head repeatedly that whole day.

The birth control pills weren't a problem; the Chicago fertility clinic wrote me a prescription that I was able to have filled that same day when we returned to Orlando. Susan and Jeff had ordered the remaining medications that I was required to take through an outside pharmaceutical company and had it all delivered to my house.

*I guess there was more homework to do than I had ever imagined,* I thought as I opened up the first pack.

Week after week, I progressively added more medicine to the regimen. First I just took birth control pills, then shots of estrogen called Lupron using a small diabetic-type needle. Then, in addition to the shots, I wore estrogen patches continuously but changed them out on a rotating schedule. Throw suppositories of more hormones in the mix three times a day to manipulate the uterine lining to become as receptive as required for the impending in-vitro transfer! My head was spinning, but knowing how important the cause was and having the support of my husband and family kept me grounded.

Upon review of the matrix of instructions in the fertility center in Chicago, I did not realize that there were two internal sonogram sessions about two and four weeks into the process to make sure I was on the proper path and had the most receptive conditions possible to receive the embryo at the transfer date. It seemed to me that the purpose of the whole process was to thin out the lining of the uterus and then hormonally manipulate my body to create the most receptive condition as possible. The thing was, my agency didn't give me a heads-up on the two transvaginal sonograms, and I was unsure where these internal sonogram procedures would be performed. I continued to give my agency the benefit of the doubt, but I knew that I should not have been in a position to ask them if the appointments had been arranged for me, and if so, where they would be held. I was told I'd receive a call from my liaison with the details. Luckily I was informed that the agency made arrangements for me to have the procedure performed in Orlando at one of their affiliated fertility clinics. Thankfully, the fertility clinic in Orlando would transfer the results to Chicago.

To keep myself on schedule, I just used the spreadsheet that the Chicago clinic sent home with me on the initial visit and kept it with me wherever I went. By the end of it all, those pages ended up really dog-eared!

That printout was all I ever used though. I was satisfied it worked out.

Phew! As if I didn't know before, I was full-speed ahead with the surrogacy.

# Chapter 7

# SUSAN

My belly and thighs were bruised from shots, and I had put on some extra pounds from the hormones. Yep, it was about to be time for the first egg retrieval! This retrieval didn't have to coincide with Heidi's readiness, as they would freeze any viable embryos we had and, when thawed, put in the best looking ones. I can't remember the exact date of my first retrieval, but boy was I nervous! I found comfort by comparing notes with a friend of mine whose fertility treatments coincided with mine.

"This is all so strange!" she said.

"The wonders of modern science!" I added.

Twice a week I had to go for monitoring and measurements of my ovaries. They could actually count the follicles and see how many eggs I was producing and how large they were. When they saw a good number that were big enough, they scheduled retrieval, and off I went.

"All you have to do is 'do it' in a cup," I told Jeff with a pout.

He snorted and replied, "Well, I don't envy you."

They had to knock me out for the retrieval. I always joked that I enjoyed the countdown part of being under anesthesia. For those ten seconds, the suspense of being unable to stop what was about to happen was a rush, as well as an opportunity to let everything go for a minute. Before I could even remember going "out," I was back in recovery. Jeff's face, more like streaks of color, slowly united and solidified in front of me. Within minutes, they were reporting how many good eggs they harvested and would let us know the three and five-day fertilization results and freeze those that were viable.

As we drove home, I was quite groggy from the anesthesia and *hungry*! I asked Jeff stop for some sandwiches and continued to nap in the car. As we headed down our street, nearing our home, my eyes were still at half-mast. I heard Jeff "ugh" under his breath and say, "Honey, open your eyes."

As I did, I saw three bright, smiling faces holding a bouquet of pink and blue balloons.

I turned to Jeff. "Is that my family?"

"Yes," he said.

We both grinned at each other at the typical "Place-family goofiness" that my family would be there just to congratulate us on the "harvest."

"Imagine what they will do if we actually end up pregnant!" I said. We giggled, pulled into the driveway, and hugged them all.

On to the waiting!

I remember while going through the rounds of hormone therapy one particular Saturday morning. We didn't have kids yet, so sleeping in was a luxury. I woke up first and headed downstairs. As Jeff headed down shortly after me, he heard the clashing of pots and pans against the stove and countertop.

"What are you doing?" he asked.

There he saw my tear-streaked, plum face as I sat in front of my farce of a breakfast. "I can't make these damned fried eggs!" I said. "They won't come out right!"

Jeff watched as I slammed the frying pan against the garbage to toss them out and continued sobbing. His eyebrows rose. "Susan. Calm. Down! It's not a big deal!"

He got a little frustrated with me as I argued otherwise. "Get ahold of yourself!" he said.

*Crash!*

I dropped the frying pan and looked back up at him, square in the eye. He later said it looked like lasers would spontaneously shoot out of my eyes with how pinpointed and intense my stare was.

"Jeff, don't you think that logically, I *know* I shouldn't be so pissed off about these eggs? I know exactly why I feel this way. If I could control it so you could have a better Saturday morning and so we could have these stupid fried eggs, don't you think I would? Can you just let me have this breakdown, *please?*"

He backed away from me and toward the stove, "Okay, but can't I just make the eggs for us?"

We knew the end result would make my messy behavior worth it. Jeff was a champ though—there were many times I didn't even want to be around *myself.*

❖

The first results yielded about seven embryos. Five good and two not so good. The next evaluation would be when they thawed them: Which ones would survive? They would take the two best ones from that point, and off we'd go!

Most people we told our story to as it was unfolding thought it was such an interesting and incredible endeavor. Of course, we'd hear our fair share of "What if this all goes wrong" questions and "What if Heidi tries to take your babies after they are born"—surrogacy-gone-bad possibilities. For the most part, people just wanted to know more and more.

Then there was the stern two cents: "That's just not natural! Test tube babies...and putting them in another woman? God didn't intend that." My response as a person who believes in God would always be, "The God I believe in created the wonderful minds that can use technology and science to help build families. He doesn't judge those who can't, and certainly not those who want to help. I know He provided this angel to us. If I can't grow our children myself, this has gotta be the next best thing—the only thing." After all, we had the ingredients but just needed the oven.

From that point, we just had to wait for Heidi to be ready, and we would hopefully "knock her up."

# Chapter 8

# *HEIDI*

On a rainy Orlando day, we were heading to Chicago for the big day we had been waiting for. The end of the month and a half of prep work was culminating with the transfer day! Each prepared schedule had the transfer date listed out as soon as you start that cycle, so from day one of the protocol, I knew exactly which day the in-vitro transfer would be.

With the transfer date already being set for everyone in their clinic who's on the same cycle, it's an extremely regimented routine. If any tiny detail does not fit, you're bumped off and have to wait for the following cycle. If you intend to try again, you would have to start back at the beginning of the month-and-a-half prep.

As a result of that process, it had been challenging to follow through with the complete schedule, but that was done and the fruits of our labors were hopefully on their way. The transfer required that I would have to have bed rest for three days after the procedure, and Susan and Jeff graciously offered for us to stay at their home during that stretch of time because it would be performed in Chicago.

"Well, I'll obviously be coming with you," said Rusty.

I smiled appreciatively before my daughter piped up from upstairs. "I want to come too!"

Rusty and I looked at each other as she skipped down the stairs. "I want to see what all goes on with this."

"What do ya think, Mama?" asked Rusty as Cayla looked at us expectantly.

The answer was simple as I saw Cayla's face alight with curiosity. Having my family's support meant everything to me. Involving herself was the truest form of that.

Meeting Susan's family was like meeting Susan with twenty times the energy. Onlookers must have thought we were at a family reunion; they warmly welcomed Rusty, Cayla, and I without hesitation.

As I gauged our reception, I saw Susan's parents standing near us, unable to stop smiling, along with her sister and brother-in-law. In spite of how difficult it sometimes is for people to wrap their heads around the procedure, I saw nothing less than abject acceptance of the way things stood. It's hard to find the exact words to describe how happy her family was to learn that all four of us, with the inclusion of their doctors at the fertility clinic, were already in the process of bringing Susan and Jeff's biological child into their lives.

"Thank you," I remember her mother telling me, covering my hand with both of hers. Her eyes brimmed with emotion as she gave my hand an affectionate squeeze. Susan's father needed no words. I met few people that looked as genuinely kind as he did. His gratitude simply overflowed in his accepting smile.

The dinner was lively and without a single moment of silence. If people weren't talking, they were listening to someone who immediately filled the gap. I stole bites in between answering questions, smuggling a bite of pasta toward my lips. Glancing to the end of the table, I saw Susan's father deep in conversation with my daughter. She was nodding and engagingly tilting her chestnut head to the side as he spoke.

"I love that book!" she said. "I read it all the time as a kid. Susan has good taste."

"Susan must've asked me to read it to her every night," he said. "Every single night, sometimes multiple times!"

Smiling, I knew we all fit right in.

The car ride to the fertility clinic where the in-vitro transfer was scheduled was enjoyable—Jeff and Susan up front and our daughter, my husband, and I in the backseat. Everyone seemed to be relaxed and anticipatory at the same time. Everything felt like it was falling into place with no pressure, even though each one of us were unsure what to expect when we arrived.

*Now if only I could go to the bathroom,* I thought, shifting in my car seat. The month and a half medicine protocol ended with one Valium and instructions to sip about a quart of water on the way to the procedure. The full bladder allowed for the best possible placement of the catheter used for the embryo transfer.

"Sorry about driving over the bumps," Jeff said, laughing at my contorted face in the rearview mirror. With each bump in the road, I worried I wouldn't be able to hold it all in any longer.

Once we all converged in the waiting room, I dwelled on the sense of déjà vu—I was in a clinic, reading the same magazine as when I discovered the agency during my daughter's appointment. There we were, full circle, hopefully approaching the crescendo of the journey together as we sat fidgeting in the waiting room. (No one fidgeted more than me! Each minute passed by painfully slow.)

With heightened senses, we all but jumped up from our chairs when the door opened to the back rooms, and they called us back. There would only be room for one more person aside from Susan and I. She glanced at Rusty, who was still sitting down when the rest of us popped up.

"Are you sure you don't want to come too?"

"I'll wait right here. Take care of Heidi back there, Jeff!"

"I guess it makes sense…Jeff and I are the ones knocking her up!" Susan joked.

We shared a chuckle before we headed toward the nurse.

"I'll see you guys soon," I told Rusty and my daughter, who shot me a thumbs up.

The three of us were brought into a small examining room that lacked the normal table. Instead, there was a big chair in the center of the room that looked like it could be used for birthing. I was given a medical gown to change into, and Jeff and Susan were asked to follow a medical professional into another area. Within a few minutes, someone was checking in on me and directed me to gather my belongings and follow them to a different examining room, which was set up with the same type of huge chair in the middle. This room had three walls and a curtain that was drawn across after I was shown in.

"Have a seat, and someone will be with you shortly."

Glancing at the clock, I started squeezing my legs together. Twenty minutes passed, and there I was thinking it was an eternity! I entertained myself by quietly listening to the couple on the opposite end of the curtain that were preparing for a transfer themselves.

"I can't believe this," I heard the female say. I imagined her and her husband interlocking hands. Able to relate on some levels with what they had been through, I had compassion for their journey to get to that point. When they left, I continued sitting, rocking back and forth and hoping the nurse didn't forget about me.

After thirty minutes, I heard what sounded like someone settling in a desk on the other side of the curtain.

"Hello, Mrs. Smith. I wanted to update you on the progress of your current retrieval. Fourteen eggs were gathered, seven viable, and four survived the frozen state. If you have any questions feel free to call us back at…"

Craning my ear to hear better, I completely forgot my impatience. I heard the clicking of buttons yet again as she left more messages, time after time again. She must have made fifteen calls in a row. So many lives were waiting on that call, so many hopes and dreams hanging on each of the calls she was making! At the same time, I was realizing that this was just one of so many clinics in the world. It was all hitting me at once how this procedure is relatively new in the medical field. The very first baby born through these procedures was only twenty-nine years old. How far science and society's acceptance had come in such a short amount of time…

In that realm of thought, I distracted myself enough to where I only zoned back in when a head peeked through the door. I looked at the prominent clock on the wall—it had been forty-five minutes!

"Okay, Heidi. Showtime! Follow me."

Our journey was coming to a crescendo!

I waddled into the room like a circus clown because I needed to pee so badly. Meanwhile I was able to perceive that Jeff and Susan could barely contain their excitement once their hairnets and hospital gowns were on. In spite of our lack of sleep, the energy sustained us in the moment as if we had drunk a whole coffee pot apiece. For me, it must have been something like twelve pots. I grimaced as I hoisted myself on the table, holding my lower stomach in discomfort.

"I can barely get up—the pee is in the way."

Much needed comic relief. We laughed again before they hoisted me up one more time.

As I settled myself on the table, Susan gave me a giddy smile and said, "This is where the magic happens!" I could barely believe we had arrived at that moment!

The doctors moved deftly while still managing to lighten the mood for everyone and ensure an even better experience. Lots of smiles and laughter circulated within the room as all the doctors and nurses were moving around as a choreographed dance performed with such delicate precision; it was impressive to watch and made the event all the more poignant. We had negotiated in our contract that we would transfer no more than two eggs because that is what was advised, in their medical professional's ethical opinion, although we could have considered a different number. The two fertilized eggs were waiting in a special room. Once we all saw the two embryos on the monitor, we couldn't take our eyes off of it. Every step of taking the eggs up into the catheter was projected onto the monitor for Jeff, Susan, and me to watch.

*Wow. These two tiny little structures have the potential to become children.* The rest was in God's hands. I could tell everyone was amazed, excited, hopeful, and nervous all at once.

"All right, watch closely," the doctor said. The embryos were brought over, then the doctor sucked them into the tiniest of syringes, inserted a catheter, and swooshed them in. We saw everything on a monitor and saw the flash across the screen as the transfer was performed.

"So that was it?" Jeff asked. We were almost in disbelief. It was only a two-minute process at most!

"Suck, insert, *swish, boom, boom, boom*—now the waiting begins," said Susan. "If only we could fast forward time to get to the next exciting part of the process."

"Guys." I had to change the subject. "Can I…"

"Yes, go ahead," said the nurse with a knowing smile. Susan says I must have turned yellow I had to pee so badly.

*Outta my way, I gotta go, move, move, move!*

After two minutes of sheer relief, I walked back into the room, still in the gown, and glad I could think straight.

*What next?* I found no one left in the room. I was probably looking like a lost puppy in a hospital gown because a nurse passed me by and said that I could get changed back into my clothes.

"What happens next?" I asked.

"You will have a pregnancy test in two weeks," she responded as if I should have already known "what happens next."

"So how do I get the test results back to you?" I asked. As dumb as it may sound, I had the impression that I would just go home and get an over-the-counter pregnancy test and call in the results to the fertility clinic. Thankfully she didn't lose her patience with me, but it seemed she had to make an effort not to do so. She softened even more after she learned I was from another state and was not planning on going to their clinic for the pregnancy test, so she had paperwork drawn up for me to take home to bring to the lab collection facility with instructions to send the results back to the clinic in Chicago on the same day. Again, the timely procedures…and should I keep mentioning the lack of "heads-up" on all the specifics from my agency?

Reuniting the five of us in the car once again was interesting to hear everyone's takes on such a unique experience. I was mostly amazed to learn that during the forty-five minutes that I was alone in the examining room, Susan and Jeff were consulting with their reproductive endocrinologist and learning the fate of their embryos that they had frozen. Alarmingly, they had started somewhere in the area of seventeen frozen that had to be thawed, leaving approximately nine that survived. Then they had to be grown to five days for the transfer because they were frozen at three days old. Once they were allowed to grow, only two survived and were viable for the transfer.

My head was spinning when I heard this.

"You're telling me that after all we've been through with the month-and-a-half prep, all this waiting, we could have reached this point only to have had *no eggs* survive for the transfer at all?" Hearing and learning this part of the procedure could not have put more of an emphasis on how delicate all of this scientific work is and who is actually in command of life. Science and society have come so far in such a short period of time, yet there is still the unknown element making it all work.

We would just have to trust that unknown element once again to make our miracle come true.

Heidi and her daughter came for a visit while I
was still on maternity leave to see how Payton
and Jordan were growing, 3 months old

Payton and Jordan at 6 months

Our 3 growing boys, Payton and Jordan at 3 months and
Farley at 1 year, this was our 2008 Christmas card photo

At the shower my sister, mom and Aunt Carol
threw, they kept me well hydrated with cocktails

Two of my best friends kiss my empty "pregnant" belly and
feed me a beer at the couples baby shower they threw

Family portrait 2011, the boys were 3
years old, Farley was almost 4

Heidi and Rusty came in a day early to spend some quality time with Payton and Jordan before their crazy 1 year party

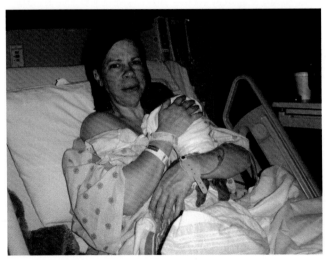

Still caring for our new arrivals in the
hospital, Heidi gently comforted Payton

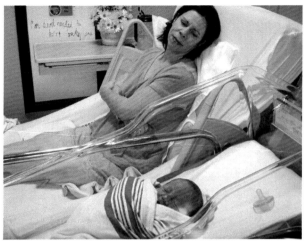

Jordan needed a couple of days with the special light because of his bilirubin levels, again, Heidi watching over the beautiful gift she gave us

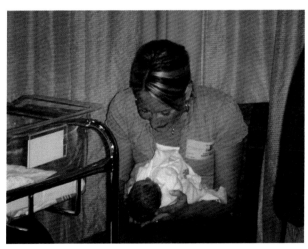

Every moment in the hospital seemed surreal, looking down at Jordan I was speechless

For so many years I never thought it possible, but
here I was, Payton and Jordan 7 months old and me 7
months into Motherhood on my first Mother's Day.

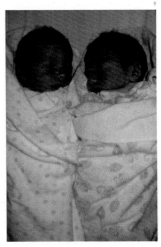

Snug as bugs in a rug getting wrapped and ready to leave
the hospital Jordan on the right, Payton on the left

The day we left the hospital with our precious
miracles, the first family photo including our
2 new family members, Rusty and Heidi

After a visit in February of 2012, Payton and Jordan began
to recognize Uncle Rusty and his eye patch
so upon their return home Rusty sent a special
package in the mail which included 2 eye patches

My mom took the whole family to Disney for Payton and
Jordan's 4th birthday, Heidi knew our intentions
of flying out of Midway and surprised us by changing
her flights so she could be on our plane

16 months old and very active, Payton and Jordan would
climb into their rocker for story time each night

# Chapter 9

# SUSAN

After the long-awaited moment that lasted a total millisecond, and a trip to the bathroom and changing back into regular clothes, we ventured back to our house for some binge relaxation. Per doctor's orders, Heidi was to do nothing for a couple of days, so we made sure she got her feet up. She was grinning like the Cheshire cat at this part of the process—just what she had been waiting for! We got some movies, made sure she had what she needed to take her medicines she was to continue taking, and we all tried to relax and not think about *it*.

"Time for chillaxin' central on the Bowen's couch," I announced. ("Chillaxin'" is a term I first learned from Heidi's daughter and was intent on using it whenever possible in the future.) "What would you like, my queen?"

Heidi was propped up on pillows and Jeff graciously conceded the remote control for her use. "I'm actually doing okay! Just go about your day as normal."

"Well, I'll make some tacos for dinner. How about that?"

God only knows how those tasted—my mind was certainly elsewhere.

Later that day, I rummaged through some mail when I found something for Heidi's daughter, Cayla. The return address was from my dad. Smiling, I could only wonder what he was up to.

"Here you go," I said casually. "You got mail too!"

Cayla's face revealed the questions popping up in her mind as she hesitantly took the envelope from my outstretched hand. When she tore it open, she held up a big Xeroxed sheet and smiled.

"What's that?" Heidi asked.

"Oh, this is the story Mrs. Bowen's dad and I talked about at dinner," she said with a giggle.

My heart swelled with pride. My dad...he was always surprising people and making them smile whenever he could.

"That's so thoughtful," said Heidi. She looked genuinely touched. "It feels good knowing that this child will have such amazing grandparents."

Somehow, in spite of the fact we had only known each other for a few months, we felt like family.

Soon it was time for them to leave and get back to regular life. We took them to the airport, hugged our good-byes (I tried not to squeeze too hard because I didn't want the embryos to pop out), and off they went.

"Thanks for all the hospitality," Heidi said, holding her suitcase with both hands.

I could only smile at the small, kind woman in front of me. What a saint. I hoped that the next time

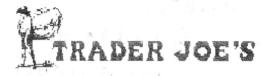

# TRADER JOE'S

4545 Fauntleroy Way SW
West Seattle WA 98126
Store #157 - (206) 913-0013

OPEN 8:00AM TO 9:00PM DAILY

| | |
|---|---|
| EGGS LRG WHT DOZ | 1.99 |
| SWEET CRISP CORN | 0.89 |
| BEANS BLACK | 0.89 |
| R-SALAD ORGANIC HERB 5 OZ | 1.99 |
| MINI-PEARL TOMATOES.. | 2.49 |
| CHEDDAR NEW ZEALAND SHARP | 3.07 |
| R-MUSHROOMS WHITE BUTTON 8 OZ | 1.69 |
| A-GINGER FRESH 4 OZ | 1.39 |
| MEAT BEEF CONV BOOL KOGI (12/ | 12.82 |

| | |
|---|---|
| SUBTOTAL | $27.22 |
| TOTAL | $27.22 |
| CASH | $40.00 |
| CHANGE | $12.78 |

ITEMS 9                                      P, Nicole
10-24-2014  02:19PM  0157 01 2278 2189

THANK YOU FOR SHOPPING AT
TRADER JOE'S
www.traderjoes.com

- Being lied to sucks.
- Being lied to after what was supposed to be something good makes everyone feel bad.
- What do I have if I can't have one boundary to myself?

we saw her, she would be a lot bigger—just around the midsection!

After she, Rusty, and Cayla walked to their terminal, it was time for ten days of waiting. For me, that was a step below eternity.

When the fateful day came, the simple act of focusing was a massive undertaking. Tapping my pen on the desk, I glanced at the clock. Only 9:52 AM. Redirecting my attention on the computer, I tried to focus on work. Somehow I ended up staring at the phone instead of the screen. Then out the window at the gray puffs of rainclouds and the inquisitive bird on the windowsill.

*Focus, Susan. If you think about other things, time will go by faster.*

Once I got bored enough with my maddening thoughts, I returned full attention to the computer. After completing a task, I granted myself one more peek at the clock. Ten twelve? You had to be kidding me! It was going to be a long day.

Time only seemed to move further backward the longer the day dragged on. Finally, the phone rang. Within a second, it was off the table and against my ear.

"Hello?"

"Hey, Susan." It was Jeff.

"Way to get my hopes up," I said. "What's going on?"

Unbeknownst to me, Jeff and Rusty made an agreement that whatever results came in, he would call Jeff first so he could then transmit the information to me.

"So Rusty told me the news," he began. I thought I would go numb from how nervous I was. And there it was…hormone levels were too low, no pregnancy. The feelings that washed over me are indescribable. Part of me was expecting a negative result, but of course, most of me hoped for positive. All I knew was that something within me crumbled and left me feeling devastated. Before I knew it, tears were falling, and Jeff and I were consoling each other.

"But it's just the first try," I reminded myself. "We will get it next time, right?"

Jeff agreed. With our focus on the next steps, our hope was renewed. That was what propelled me forward. I knew my insurance would cover three more retrievals and unlimited transfers, so we'd definitely try a second time, but our contract with Heidi stated we would transfer up to two embryos three times. Three times was our line in the sand, and we all knew it but we kept our eyes on the next steps always.

When I came home, I leaned back in the chair as Snickers poked his head by my legs. I took comfort in his large, glossy eyes and pet his head. His tail wagged at my touch and slightly cheered me. As we sat together, I realized I should call Heidi. I knew this had to be hard on her too. She got herself ready emotionally and physically to take on the charge and responsibility of growing our potential child, and she must have felt deflated too.

"Hello?" her voice sounded muffled on the other line.

"Hi, there, Heidi." Before long, we both unloaded into a disappointed, tearful conversation for a few minutes, understanding where each of us were coming from and how the other must be feeling. We were on the same page and assured that no one was at fault.

"Well, at this point we have to pull ourselves up from our bootstraps and continue on," I said, dabbing my eye with a Kleenex.

"This will help us appreciate round two even more, I think," said Heidi. I was sure she was right.

Just the next day, I contacted the doctor and began readying myself for the next attempt as Heidi did the same. Levels were checked, meds were ordered, and off we went for round two.

Heidi kept me updated. Everyone was given instructions from our Chicago fertility clinic on when to start the next round of medication. The clinic's cycles are very regulated, and if you do not start from the beginning along with everyone else on the current timeline, then you have to wait until the next cycle starts (about every two months). It is a precise and multifaceted event. Heidi was forwarded a timetable that was on par with the last medication cycle that she had just finished and all the medicine was mailed to her house on time.

There were also the two monitoring visits where your uterine lining is measured to show you are within range of creating the best receptive conditions for the in-vitro transfer. The first visit measures that your lining has thinned out then the second shows it's built up to their manipulation specifications.

Well, that was that. The past was behind us, and we were full speed ahead. By this time, I was a pro at giving myself my own shots, and Heidi was an expert in everything.

"Back to the pills, then pills and shots, then pills and shots and patches, shots, patches, and suppositories, and so on and so on," Heidi had said good naturedly.

One brisk autumn day, a friend and I decided to raid the pumpkin patch. Our faces were flushed and our lips chapped as we walked back toward the parking lot. Right before I opened the car door, I received a call. Caller ID said it was the agency.

"Hey, hold on just a sec," I told my friend. I answered the phone expecting an update on escrow and finances and next steps in general, nothing too heavy as there were always details to wrap up.

"Hey there," I said. "What's going on?"

"Well, Susan, there's a lot going on."

*Oh boy.*

All she said to me was that Heidi could no longer be our surrogate. She was deemed "ineligible" due to fibroid tumors that were discovered, and we would now have to start from scratch to look for a new surrogate.

I felt like I was hit by a semi. Forgetting to breathe, I whispered, "Okay, well what can we do?"

Abruptly and abrasively she didn't hesitate to let us know that we wouldn't be refunded any of our agency fees if we decided against going forward with another surrogate from the agency. If we stayed with the agency, we would have another stipend to pay as well. I wish I could say I was exaggerating this call for dramatic purposes in the book, but I kid you not. To this day, I remember it vividly as if it were a bad dream.

When I hung up, I could feel the color draining from my face. Staring at my shoes and the crunchy orange and brown leaves around it, I tried to blink away the tears—unsuccessfully. There I was in public, bawling my eyes out. Children lugging around bowling ball-sized pumpkins looked at me with alarm as their mothers gently pushed them along. That only made it worse.

"Susan, Susan, what happened?" my friend said. "Let's get in the car and talk about it."

She could totally relate; she was the friend who was going through fertility herself. She knew all too well the ups and down of the process. I was just told to forget about everything we had accomplished over the last ten months, that it was time to start from scratch, and to cough up an additional 20K. She felt my pain.

My intent in this memoir is not to focus on the money parts—it's all worth it in the end, but understand that even with the insurance coverage I had (which had excellent out-of-pocket expenses for Jeff and I), everything totaled over 70K for this entire thing. That's with the assistance of Heidi flying free and being so willing to use her vacation time for days off related to all of this. She never even charged us back for that, which she would have been completely within her full rights to do.

That was only one small reason why that phone call was jarring. So at this point, having already spent over 30K and the owner asking us for another 15K to start over when we hadn't even begun the really expensive parts was beyond logic to me.

(Also I'd like to note that Heidi's "fee" for carrying and delivering us two healthy boys was a drop in the bucket compared to the other expenses. We said on more than one occasion that it seemed like the money was dog-eared for so many other people and not Heidi. My hand to God, if I win the lottery, the first million I get is going to Heidi. I can never repay her for what she did for us, and what we did pay her was a pittance when you think of everything she did—and I know, it's in writing now for the whole world to see, but I can't put a price tag on what she did for us. Unfortunately the likelihood of winning the lottery is slim—sorry, Heidi.)

Unable to believe we'd be at a stopping point after only one try, I frantically called our doctor for another opinion. He wanted to see Heidi, and I called her to see if she would consider a recheck with our clinic. She of course did, and we got that scheduled straight away.

In the meantime, though, being so invested in helping us create our family, Heidi and Rusty told us of a relative of theirs who might be willing to "take it from here" and serve as a potential new surrogate. They didn't want to see us back at the starting line. Can you imagine? Not only had Heidi offered to be our surrogate, but she and Rusty had gone on the hunt for a replacement—even set up a call for me to talk to this wonderful volunteer. Everything was happening at such a pace that it all became a blur…life became a blur.

As devastating and shocking as it was, we were not going to give up on this. Neither were they.

# Chapter 10

# HEIDI

I had learned that I could have the laboratory blood work done for the pregnancy test at a local hospital. After the ten days following my return from Chicago, I figured I'd give the hospital's lab a try. During the blood draw the woman technician and I struck up a conversation, she was really nice and helpful and informed me that if I wanted to, I could come back later that day for the results in writing. Not wanting to miss that opportunity after all we had waited for, I strode into the lab office of the hospital feeling at ease and was handed a sealed envelope from the technician. She informed me that the results were faxed back as requested to the fertility clinic. I thanked her and went on my way toward my car. Everything seemed to be falling into place finally.

When I opened the envelope in the parking lot on my way to my car, something did fall: it was both my jaw and my heart sinking right into my stomach!

*Negative? How in the world could this be negative?* I have always fit the fertile myrtle nickname. There was never a need to "try" when it came to creating my family; it just happened. With all the assistance we had from such a scientific procedure, how in the world did this fail to happen?

The farther I drove, the more my sense of inadequacy rose. I was letting a lot of people down, and the disbelief was a hard pill to swallow. Each time my car slowed down to a stop at the light, I gripped my hands on the steering wheel and let my forehead sink against it as the reality of the situation engulfed me.

Having already let the agency know that Rusty and I would break the news to Susan and Jeff, I wondered how I would do it. No one could blame me for my anxiety surrounding the call, so Rusty took the lead in that situation and made sure to contact Jeff so he could figure out a way to approach Susan about the negative result from our first try.

As the day went on, our despair turned to anger and pity for the Bowens.

*There are so many children that are born to families that do not appreciate their children or fill the responsibilities that parenting requires, but this couple will make such great parents! It's so unfair!* I thought while grocery shopping. I mechanically extracted each product from the shelf, scarcely knowing what I would be purchasing.

Thankfully, as you know, Susan was compassionate and wanted to try again. I had come out of that conversation feeling much more confident and that nothing worth having comes easy.

On to try number two! Back on the saddle and on their fertility clinic's timetable. All was feeling very familiar and seemed to be progressing smoothly.

But then there was the discovery of the situation with the fibroids. What the . . .?

That day, I had my last internal monitoring visit. The first monitoring visit of the cycle was to make sure everything was on track before meeting up again in a few weeks. During the second monitoring visit of the second cycle, which was just one week away from the date of the second in-vitro transfer, the agency-referred technician who had performed the past three visits I had in this same office in Orlando started slowing down and looking concerned.

"Hm, I'll be right back," she said, pushing her chair back and exiting the examining room. She came back not long after and delivered the news without much emotion.

"It seems you have fibroids and you'll have to contact your clinic. You're not a candidate for surrogacy anymore." She did not even look me in the eye. I was dumbfounded. Okay, actually more than that, I was ready to blow! I was all hormoned-up after having manipulated my system with so many types of medication for weeks on end. Normally I'm pretty even-keeled, but I was having a hard time restraining myself. *What the heck is going on,* I wondered, but I knew that this technician didn't deserve me to unload on her; she was just doing her job, so I just got dressed and walked out feeling very inadequate and robotic in my state of shock yet again.

I had to work that day so I went directly from that appointment to the Orlando airport, completely unsure of what had just taken place and how to fix it. While I was walking out of the airport in Detroit after a full day of flying with my colleagues, heels clacking against the pavement as we walked to the hotel shuttle, I whipped out my phone and turned it on to call the agency. Unfortunately, they hadn't responded to the voicemail I had left earlier. For five whole minutes, I was on hold before the liaison answered.

"I guess because you have fibroids in your uterine lining, the fertility clinic said you are not a candidate to be a surrogate by their standards anymore."

*Tell me something I don't know,* I thought ruefully.

"But don't worry," she continued. "The owner of the agency has already spoken with the intended parents." If her intention was to make me feel better, it backfired on her because I felt worse tenfold! It may have been selfish of me, but I couldn't help think. "You found the time to call Susan and Jeff but did not have the time to leave me even a voicemail saying 'sorry it didn't work out'?"

During my overnight I tossed and turned in my sheets. Unable to watch television or focus on much of anything, I decided to get out my laptop and write a much needed scathing e-mail to the owner of the agency. Too long had I remained quiet. Too long had I let their lack of professionalism throw me under the bus. Knowing that there was not one person who worked in that office who had carried out or participated in being a surrogate, I took a leap of faith and assumed that no one who worked there could relate with the extent of hurtful feelings their lack of communication added to this experience. I gave constructive criticism of how to deal with such an issue should it ever arise for them in the future.

So that was it? Our journey would come to a screeching halt, we'd say, "Well, thanks anyway," and part ways, just like that? The prospect was making the initial negative response from our first try pale in comparison to how much this turn of events burnished my ego and hurt to deal with.

For days I was on autopilot; I hugged myself in my sweatshirt and desperately tried to make sense of the flurry of emotions that were rendering me, unable to listen to anyone or do anything. Imagining Susan's bright, laughing face and her and Jeff's hospitality, I felt unbearably guilty. When Cayla had received the Xeroxed sheets from that book in the mail from Susan's dad, right then and there, I had such a warm feeling wash over me, reassuring me that I was doing the right thing for the right family and that this child would be well taken care of.

I had no idea what Susan's reaction would be, but I knew I had to e-mail her. Unlatching my clammy hands from each other, I nervously typed up a quick e-mail stating that I wish I could have a better explanation as to why the rug was being pulled out from under their feet again so abruptly, but I had not noticed anything different from the last round. If I had, then I would have taken immediate action. No matter how they were taking it, I knew it was best that we give each other space so we could digest the current state of affairs.

As I reflected back on those events while I sat on the computer, having sent Susan the e-mail about the fibroids situation, I reminded myself of the decision that distance could be the best medicine. I was the surrogate that failed after all. Resting my cheek on my fist, I started to wallow in such self-pity and pity for the couple I was beginning to love. I had retreated so far within myself that I didn't even hear my phone buzzing as Rusty called me. Upon seeing his missed call, I straightened up and scooped up my phone to call back.

"Heidi, why not set up an appointment with the gynecologist? I mean *your* gynecologist," he said after my summary of how I felt after all the disappointments.

"Why should I do that?" I asked softly.

"See if there's anything that should be addressed now that you know you have fibroids in your uterine lining."

"Oh, good point."

Luckily, I was able to get an appointment as soon as I returned from my work trip. The doctor gave me the same internal sonogram that they had performed at the other fertility clinic that deemed me ineligible for surrogacy. Watching the doctor's face for a clue, he maintained an impassive countenance. I would have to wait for his words.

"Well, Heidi," he said. I analyzed his tone—he sounded lighthearted, strangely. "I don't see any fibroids. I'm unsure as to why this clinic would have given you that diagnosis…"

What a relief! But then again, who was right? Now I felt uneasy all over. I all but held my breath until the moment the doctor conferred with the other office and compared his findings to theirs. He also said he would submit his findings to the fertility clinic in Chicago, and that if he had to make any determination, that he would stand by his findings and in his professional opinion that I was qualified to be a surrogate.

"However, the biological parents' clinic will have the final say in the matter," he added.

For the first time in weeks, I could breathe without the sensation of a tight belt binding my chest.

When we caught back up with Susan and Jeff, we let them know that my follow-up with my gynecologist showed no signs of fibroids at all and that he submitted his findings to their doctor in Chicago. Rusty and I sat erect on the couch in anticipation of their response.

"Well," Susan began, "if you are down to continue on as our surrogate, and if you're cleared, we are willing to take that route again."

"Of course I am," I said. We were in this together. I was going to help finish what we started.

"But we have a stipulation," Jeff said. "We no longer want to do business with your agency."

"Yeah…no, thank you," Susan said.

After having so many important issues fall through the cracks and feeling like I had been left on my own to figure out the process, I had no qualms about leaving my agency behind. The four of us felt confident that we had experienced enough to know what to expect and had trusted each other enough that we were willing to take the risk. Rusty and I had already been disenchanted by the agency anyway, to say the least.

There were some emotional phone calls between the owner of the surrogacy agency and me after the e-mail I had sent, but it was drowned out with all the swirling negative events taking place. For the first time in my life, I held the phone up to my ear with an irritable frown and tapped my foot. Honestly, I felt much more allegiance to the Bowens after all we had experienced together, and I did not think twice of signing whatever legal paperwork was drawn up to end our contract with my agency.

During the time prior to the next cycle, I went to request the medical records from my monitoring clinic visits and was astonished to learn that I did not have a legal right to the records because they were not mine—they were the property of my agency who arranged the visits. HIPAA laws prevented me from obtaining medical records of procedures that were performed on me because they were facilitated by and paid for by the egg donation and surrogacy agency, so they were "their" medical records. My innate nature to not push issues took hold again, and I let out a deep breath.

"Pick your battles, Heidi," I reminded myself. In the end, I had more important matters to deal with: getting a Bowen baby born independently.

# Chapter 11

# SUSAN

As Heidi, Rusty, Jeff, and I continued on as a tight-knit band of baby makers, we hoped the worst was behind us.

While investigating what may have happened and the monitoring that Heidi was getting in Florida, we found a mismanagement of our escrow funds had occurred, and we had even less now in that fund than we thought. Here I was being asked to forfeit the entire agency fee and start over and then to find out that Heidi could indeed continue, yet we hadn't been told everything as far as how our funds were managed and what they were used for.

"It's not like this is an inexpensive endeavor!" Jeff raged. "How can they do this?"

"I'll be a lot more confident moving on without them," I said. Sure, we'd lose the fee, but they were going to revoke that anyway just by the mere incidence that Heidi wasn't deemed acceptable to move ahead after finding the fibroid cyst. We decided that with the legal contract in place and all of us being protected by our attorneys on either side should something go awry, we'd take this Bowen baby-making business into our own hands.

Right as we were full speed ahead, my mother called. "We'd like for you to come over later," she said.

"Yeah, sure. Anything going on?"

"Oh, just something to talk about."

*Huh, that's funny* was just about all I thought. No worries had crept through my mind.

I walked into the house expecting to smell the familiar aroma of my mom's hearty homemade cooking, but instead, they were sitting on the couch with the television even turned off. My dad, stone-faced, was the first to turn to me.

"There's something we have to tell you," my dad began.

The news that followed was hard to handle. Cancer is an ugly word, even when it's seemingly under control. Thyroid cancer is supposed to be "curable" by basically removing the thyroid. But while going through his CAT and PET scans, the doctors were concerned that it looked like quite a bit of tumor growth around the thyroid, but again, we had been led to believe the surgery would take care of it and he'd go on thyroid medicine and all would be fine.

Unnerved, I tried not to let it slow down Jeff and I from the process at hand.

"The doctors say it's curable, just remember that," Dad said. Leaning forward and giving me a reassuring look, I could tell he didn't want me to worry. Good ol' Dad.

In November 2007, his testing and scanning and screenings started for his diagnosis, and it's when Heidi and I began prepping for a fresh transfer as well. I can't remember the exact date that his "routine removal" of his thyroid was scheduled, but when the first surgeon got in there, she swiftly realized this would not be routine.

"The mass around the thyroid is too great for me to tackle," she said. "We're going to need more tests, and I'll refer him to Northwestern Hospital." There he would have further testing and diagnosis. He was put on thyroid medicine, and his next surgery was scheduled: February 29, 2008.

My dad was always the happiest when he was around his family, but as the days grew closer to his surgery, you could see it in his eyes even more. He seemed to breathe us in more than ever, and he and my mom began to embark on the project of "adding a little *joy* to their lives every day." That statement has a dual meaning; his sister, who had passed away many years before, was named Joy, so I know he was starting to reflect on family near and beyond. He just seemed to smile a little longer and laugh a little louder than usual. He had to be scared—who wouldn't be? But he didn't talk about it. He was too much of a gentleman to ever let those kinds of conversations monopolize family time.

Around Thanksgiving of 2007, it was clear our Collie of almost twelve years was nearing the end. I'd stay up night with him holding his head up so he could breathe, and he was having trouble even getting a drink of water.

"But look at him, Jeff," I said when we discussed is health. "You would never know he's sick. He's so happy." I pointed to his clear-as-day doggie smile. In spite of everything life was hurling at him, Snickers' sunshiny outlook on life revealed itself through the tail that never quit wagging.

After a vet visit, she showed me a black and white X-ray of his lungs. They were speckled even more than last time, and the tumor was worse.

"It might be time for you to take him off of his other medicines for arthritis and just give him quality of life," the vet gently said.

My head, slumped down in sadness, suddenly snapped up. "Does that mean it's...today?"

Jeff had accompanied me, knowing I'd be a wreck without his support. He exchanged glances with the vet, and they both shook heads simultaneously. "No, no, not today," she said. I sighed in relief as I looked down at my little guy.

While I was relieved as could be, Jeff knew it wouldn't be long and that that day would have been just as good as any other. With everything else we had going on, though, the thought of losing my first dog, the one who lived so many phases of life with me—single, married, moving eight times with me neither of us were ready yet...

The very next morning, I got up early for egg retrieval monitoring. Groggy and low-spirited, Jeff and I spent the whole night listening to Snickers pace. He wasn't able to lie down for more than ten minutes at a time. His chest was collapsing. We slept on the couch in the living room to be near him all night long. I woke up and let him out the front door because those steps were easier to climb than in the back.

"Come on, buddy," I cooed. I didn't want him to sense my devastation. Snickers labored down the stairs, went pee, turned around, and looked at me as if to say, "That's it, I can't do it, I'm done." The look in his eyes was clearly of defeat.

"C-c-come on," I said. Shaken, I knew there was no conviction in my command. Snickers simply didn't want to come back up the stairs. He let his body sink to the ground as he stared at me apologetically. Before I knew it, tears stung my eyes and my throat constricted.

"Please, boy. Come back in."

Jeff watched from the couch with tears in his eyes. I turned around, bawling.

"Call the vet," I said. "It's today. He just told me."

"I know, honey. It's the right time." Jeff stood up and put his hands on my shoulders as I buried my face in my hands.

At 10:00 AM that day, when I returned, we said good-bye to the most wonderful dog in the world. He was a family member that would never be replaced.

Meanwhile, I was popping with eggs, and Heidi was ready for transfer. Through the miracle of fertility science and the skilled doctors and staff at our clinic, our next attempt was upon us that mid-December. Again, Heidi and Rusty came up for a few days, the transfer happened as swiftly as last time: two viable embryos in, quality relaxation at Casa De Bowen, and we were on our way.

*It just has to work this time*, I thought. By that point, my mind wouldn't travel down the road of the "what ifs."

Interrupting my anxiety, Jeff and I prepared for our biannual trip to Florida to visit his parents at Christmas. My parents were joining us there this year, and we were all excited for the warm holiday—a welcome change from the blustery, gray Illinois weather.

The day before we left, I was folding beach towels in my suitcase last-minute as my toiletries were spread out in a circle on the floor. Scratching out the last few items off the list with my favorite inky blue pen, I heard Jeff unlocking the front door. I tried to block out the memory of Snickers joyfully running to greet him. It would take awhile for that pain to go away.

As if on cue, Jeff lifted my spirits. "Hey, I got you something today," he said.

"Hmm, what's the occasion?"

He pulled a little white box out of his front coat pocket and extended it toward me.

"Go on," he urged with a smile.

Raising my eyebrow, I carefully lifted the box and…

"Oh my gosh. Does this mean—?"

"Yes. Yes, it does."

My joyful cries filled the room as I beheld a necklace of a little metallic mother holding a newborn baby.

# Chapter 12

# *HEIDI*

This time it felt more of a quick and smooth process. Now another two weeks' worth of anxious waiting. Everything felt easier as anything does once you're comfortable with what to expect. I was pleased with the quick service I received at the hospital's lab for the blood test, so I went back to the same one I had on our initial round. I knew I should be able to receive the results within a few hours handed to me in a sealed envelope and could not wait this time until I got out to the parking lot.

"Oh my gosh!" I gasped. "It's positive! Oh my gosh!"

I had the same technician who did the blood draw months earlier, so we had established somewhat of a rapport. I was so excited that I told her everything. "It's for a family that can't deliver on their own, so this is such wonderful news!"

She gave a genuine grin. "That's great. How heartwarming!"

Finally, we were on our way to bringing home the Bowens' baby!

"No! No, no, no, no! Oh my goodness, no! How much more can this family be expected to take? How in the world can we break this news to them, especially on Christmas Eve?" I told Rusty tearfully. We had been through enough ups and downs already during these last three rounds, but all I was thinking was that I did not want to break Susan's heart.

The technician who was beginning to know me pretty well now had informed me that when the blood hCG numbers are low, which they were, it was considered a weak pregnancy.

"That's probably why the clinic wanted an additional reading," she explained.

"Okay, thanks." I didn't have the heart to get into a deeper conversation and explain that once the result it positive, you are required to continue going back every few days for a pregnancy blood test to make sure the hCG numbers were increasing, giving the fertility clinic guidelines of what medication can be prescribed to assist nature in sustaining the growing miracle.

"Thanks for your service to our country," I said, which was my usual departing note to the former combat medic. Unsmiling, I was on my way.

We sat in silence at the dining room table upon hearing the news. "I have it taken care of," said Rusty softly a few minutes after I broke the news to him. All I could imagine was Susan and Jeff sitting dejectedly in front of their Christmas tree, the whole family silent upon gaining the news. This time would be even worse than before because they thought they had finally done it—we all had.

It was a resignation by all four of us that we would take a break during the holidays and recollect ourselves. For our final try, we agreed that if surrogacy was meant to work, it would. If the results came back negative, then we would have to accept that this journey was not meant to be ours. We were soon back in what was now a very familiar cycle starting from the beginning one last time.

We made our decision to proceed within enough time to join the very next cycle that the Chicago fertility clinic had coming up, so we were strapped in for the last turn on our emotional roller coaster ride. Of course, no attempt would be complete without some setback or drama, right? It would feel wrong without it.

Now that we were not using the monitoring clinic in Orlando for the two transvaginal mile-marker visits, Rusty and I flew to Chicago and headed to the Bowen's clinic for each of the monitoring appointments. As Rusty and I were flying into Chicago for the last appointment and were descending when the bumps, jolts, and turbulence boded ill, the intercom message filled the plane.

"This is your captain speaking. There seems to be a large storm system moving toward the airport."

When I glanced out the little round window, I saw angry black clouds. I checked my watch worriedly. Although accustomed to the sudden turn of events that air travel was subject to, I worried we wouldn't get to our final monitoring session on time. Though circling for a while, we were diverted to Columbus, Ohio. My nerves grated on me until Rusty looked at me with a shrug. There was no way we would get to an appointment on time.

"I guess all is lost," I said dejectedly as we landed at long last.

Rusty pursed his lips together before speaking. "Hmm…do you think the Chicago clinic would take the monitoring results from your ob-gyn in Orlando?"

"But can we get a visit scheduled and back to Orlando in time?"

The onslaught of questions put my mind in a flurry, so we took the plunge and decided it wouldn't hurt to ask. As crazy as it sounds, my ob-gyn was once again onboard and being accommodating toward our situation. Somehow we even made it back to Orlando in time!

Everything turned out just fine! Monitoring visit in Orlando showed to be on track, all systems go for our third and final round of trying. Next step, transfer day!

At this stage of attempts and with our history of results, Susan's endocrinologist felt comfortable suggesting we consider transferring three embryos this time instead of using two as we had on both previous attempts. "In for a penny, in for a pound" was my attitude by the time we were on our final push for pregnancy.

"It's time to put of all my eggs in one basket," Susan said.

Silly woman! "Sure, I'm game" (and happy she wasn't suggesting any more).

Everything became routine, so the one image that vividly stands out during this transfer was glancing at the three embryos in the petri dish on the monitor screen. Two were small, and then there was a super large one in the middle.

"Maybe that one grew a day extra compared to the other two," I joked. "Or it could hold twins."

We all speculated that it very well could have come from separate egg collection dates that Susan had gone through. "Wouldn't it be crazy if that were true because that big guy could actually be older than their siblings if there were multiples?" said Susan.

I hardly remember much of the other details of this transfer because, I'm sad to say, it was becoming routine by that point. What I do recall with clarity, and still feel in the nerve synapses in my left hand when I think about it, is Susan taking my hand in both of hers and giving it a squeeze right at the moment of the transfer. My heart swelled with sentiment as I realized this was our last time to transfer, and that so much depended on that very moment. I just hoped Susan would get her happy ending.

Mid-February. We were holding our breaths for a positive blood test. My heart pounded and my knees shook at the possibility of bearing bad news—that it just wasn't going to happen at all.

*Oh, gosh. I can't go down that road,* I told myself. So getting out of my car, oblivious to the world around me, I set out for the hospital lab while taking deep breaths. I barely even noticed the cars near me, or the rush and bustle once I walked inside.

When I was handed the unsealed envelope, I thought I would burst. Breath held, blue in the face, I shakily opened it. My eyes widened, and I almost dropped the envelope.

Guess what I left the hospital lab with?

"Hi, Jeff. Well guess what. We got the blood results back. We've been blessed with a positive test result!" Rusty paused with a grin as he listened to the emotional reaction on the other side. "And not only that, the numbers are a little higher this time. To the tune of being in the thousands!"

Like anyone in this day and age, when we saw the numbers, we immediately went to Google for answers. Quickly we discovered high numbers of hCGs often indicated multiple births!

*Better keep that to myself for the time being*, I thought. I knew Susan must have been cautiously optimistic at that juncture. When we next spoke, she said, "My reproductive endocrinologist suggested he would like to supplement our chances by putting you on progesterone suspended in oil to help increase the chances of sustaining this pregnancy. That's right—more shots. At least you're a pro by now!"

Oh boy, not only more shots, but this time they were not with small diabetic-type needles; this medication was injected using the intramuscular needles. In other words, these were sinister needles, a stinking inch-and-a-half-long and very thick, would impale my backside every few days.

"Yep, this is dedication to the cause!" I replied. As unlikely as it sounds, the needles actually weren't so bad. In any case, I became more proficient with them and would often administer them to myself in hotel rooms. We were already that far, so it was time to go full-speed ahead!

# Chapter 13

# SUSAN

"Oh my God! Oh my God! Oh *my God*!"

*Susan, ya gotta calm down. You know what happened last time.*

I felt bipolar. Excitement spread through me at an exponential rate and was threatening to bust out. Reason and caution tried to obstruct it with a giant mental dam, but excitement leaked out anyway. I could not believe it. After all the trouble we had gone through, and my reaction the last time, I simply couldn't believe it.

We had gotten off the plane in Florida, looking down the terminal for Jeff's parents' smiling faces. Once we found each other, my mother-in-law looked at me as if to say, "So? So? Did it work this time?" I stopped, looked at Jeff, and showed her the necklace. She squealed with glee, and we all hurried to the car.

Somewhere inside of me, and I know inside Jeff, we were cautiously optimistic. The hCG levels being reported were just enough to indicate a pregnancy, no more, no less it seemed, but they weren't saying she wasn't pregnant; so we went on each day to the next assuming eventually they would start to rise. Then, like a red sack full of coal, right there on Christmas Eve morning, Heidi told us the sad news. I absolutely lost it and during my full-on breakdown, I tortured myself with the blame game.

"It's all my fault I can't give Jeff kids or a name-sake for *his* parents," I cried. I wept and wept at the kitchen table as they all tried to console me. Then I realized I'd have to tell my parents they wouldn't be grandparents yet again. Calling them reluctantly when they were at their hotel, I told them in broken speech what had happened.

"We will be right over," Dad said. In a matter of minutes, they swooped me up and took me to breakfast. Jeff and his parents understood.

As we sat at the coffee shop, I tried to listen to them through tears. I just didn't know where or who I was anymore. What was all this for? How could I keep putting Jeff, Heidi, Rusty, and all of our friends and family through this? The pressure was mounting, and I felt dizzy. I had tried to be so realistic about the whole process, treat it like a business and always expect the worst, but deep down, that's not ever what you really think about. Your heart always wants the good news and can't help but yearn for it.

Although my parents primarily sat and listened to me cry, trying to comfort me with their presence, I was being torn limb from limb. I looked at the world with my watery lens, blinking through the tears to stare down at my mug of black coffee. The upbeat saxophone music in the background only felt like a mockery to my pain.

After untold minutes, my mom softly began to speak. "You took awhile to get here too. We had wanted a second child for a long time, and it took us four years after your sister to have you."

"It was hard," Dad said. "But we kept trying. You were worth the wait."

Of course that only caused fresh tears, but I cherish that memory to this day.

We weathered our Christmas and decided to take five for a few weeks; we were back in the game. We had extra frozen embryos from another attempt, so I stopped all of the hormones, and we put our sights on a new Great Dane puppy and a trip we had planned to Mexico with five other couples. As far as anyone else knew though, we were done trying. Having been faced twice with the horror of disappointing everyone with failed attempts (at least that is how it feels when you go through it), we decided that everything happens for a reason.

"Let's enjoy a vacation," I said. "My sights are solely on that." Snickers was gone, so we had no worries about leaving him alone in his condition. We'd wait for Heidi to be deemed ready for our third and final try (God bless her), and around Valentine's Day, we had a plan to pick up our new puppy. One might ask why during all of this we decided to get a puppy, and a Great Dane puppy at that, but we decided we needed to go on with life as if the third attempt wasn't going to work either. We had our line in the sand, and it was getting danger-ously close.

Somehow, Heidi graciously agreed to have three embryos transferred. Everything process-wise went off without a hitch as usual. And the waiting would begin....

In the meantime, we hadn't told anyone we were trying again. Not even my parents. They were readying for my father's impending surgery on February 29 and trying to enjoy each day leading up to that.

But then I received *the* call! After all the guilt, the doubt, and moving forward with our lives, it had happened! When I had told a confidant at work who had been through fertility herself, she dropped her fork over lunch and said, "Susan, that usually indicates multiples. You may not just be getting one kid."

"Holy sh—what? Is this real life?"

From that point onward, I decided we could tell people; the doctors felt confident and the numbers only continued to steadily increase. As I was driving to my parents', my friend called me.

"Hi, Swooz, its Janna. What are you up to?"

"Hey! I'm just heading over to my parents for lunch."

"On a weekday? Hmm…something special must be going on."

"Yeah, I just wanted to tell them something important and just got here, so I gotta run."

"Why are…" my friend paused for a second. "Wait, you guys are pregnant, aren't you? Oh my God!" she screamed into the phone.

To this day, I can't wrap my head around how she knew when we hadn't told a soul—I guess she could hear it in my voice and the fact I didn't want to tell her because I wanted to tell my parents first.

"Call me the minute you get back in the car!" she said. I agreed that I would.

Honestly, I don't even remember a single part of what happened at lunch or if there was even food on the table. Unable to keep it to myself a moment longer, I blurted out, "Heidi is pregnant! We finally knocked her up!"

My parents' faces melted with happiness, compassion, and love all at the same time—and then we just giggled.

"Time to crack open a few beers," I announced. They heartily agreed.

Unfortunately, the clinking of our beer bottles together in celebration was the last of our happiness as a family for a long while. Not long after that day, my dad went into surgery to remove his thyroid and all of the cancerous tumors surrounding his throat. The disease was literally choking him to death, and some lesions had also been found around his lungs (but that was reserved for a second surgery). We checked him in on February 29, and what was supposed to be a four-to-six-hour surgery turned into ten worrisome hours.

When the surgeon came out, we all put down our coffee cups and sprung to our feet.

"I wasn't able to get even half of it out," he said slowly. "It's very tangled in there."

My stomach dropped, and I could barely swallow. Instinctively, I grabbed my mom's hand. She, along with my sister and I, began to weep in relief that he was out of surgery okay while trying to disregard the sinking feeling that we were in for a tough ride.

Dad was finally out of surgery and in the ICU, where they would have to let him heal a bit before going in for more, or perhaps shrinking it with radiation before going back in. My mom's, sister's and my face just fell at the news.

Although this is a surrogacy memoir, I bring up my dad and other things that went on during that time because no matter what, life happens around us all every day. No matter what we are going through, whether it's a fertility journey, a new job, the loss of a family member, our college education, and so on, you never really get the chance to focus on one thing. While something so wonderful that we had waited and persevered for was underway, a devastating, challenging, and horrid loss awaited. Neither one could be stopped.

Our much-needed relief from the all-encompassing concern for my dad was Heidi's next visit. As my dad sat recovering from that surgery in the hospital, just days later, Heidi and Rusty came up to have the ultrasound that would show us the first glimpse of our baby.

"I'm beyond excited to see our grain of rice in our well-chosen oven," I told Heidi after hugging her. We both grinned excitedly, giddy as kids.

As we drove to the clinic, nothing felt real. Surely we were waiting for another upset. Could we really be seeing our baby after such a long and rocky road? Jeff and I braced ourselves, almost fearful of being too happy. Rusty held Heidi's hand as the ultrasound technician rubbed the cold gel on her belly. Then the wand…

"Ah! There it is!" I shouted. He or she was right there on the screen! Our little grain of rice!

"But wait, what's that?" Jeff asked.

"Another grain of rice!" I boomed.

"Twins!" added the ultrasound tech. "There are twins!"

Our excitement radiated throughout the room, but during the next pause, Jeff and I looked at each other and continued to brace ourselves.

*I don't think anyone in this room wants to see a third grain of rice*! I thought nervously. The technician thoroughly checked Heidi's belly for any more inhabitants, but phew, there were just the two.

"Oh my God, two!" I announced triumphantly. Jeff squeezed my hand so hard I thought it'd break, but I didn't care. We couldn't wait to tell everyone! The clinic was right near the hospital where my dad was so he was to be the first to know. I started making phone call after phone call to all of our friends and family. Let the planning begin!

We knew we wouldn't know the sexes of the babies until about June, but we were able to label them baby A and baby B, as the doctors and clinic told us they really wouldn't move much from their designated places, and they would be tracking the measurements and health of each one by those labels. Wow, baby A and B...initially I'd have been beside myself with glee to simply have one! Thanks to Heidi, the marvels of modern science, and God, I would be a mother—and to *two* babies!

The situation was surreal. There I was, bursting at the seams with joy, but at the same time, feeling devastated about my dad's condition. It's a feeling that, to this day, is difficult to describe. As the preparations were full swing, my father was failing faster than anyone had anticipated. The collateral damage from the first surgery left him in hospitals and rehab from February 29 until the third week of April. Sometimes we would get him home for a night or two and think, "It's all going to be fine. His spirit is bright and strong as it ever was, and he is fighting the good fight for all of us."

"Shouldn't you get home?" Dad asked as I sat up with him in the hospital late one night. He was only able to tilt his head slightly to the left, where I sat.

"Eh, I have to get used to getting little sleep for when the kiddos are here," I said. Dad nodded slowly but didn't say much. All we could hear was the beeping and technical sounds of the hospital room.

Whenever I mentioned the kids, they were somber moments. Perhaps he felt he wouldn't be here to meet the babies or, rightfully so, was concentrating on his own battle and recovery with cancer. I truly thought for a while that although his recovery was much longer than anticipated, there was just no way he wouldn't be here to meet our new arrivals, let alone take us on the Disney trip he and my mom were already talking about for when the twins turned four. The doctors and oncologists tried radiation therapy and were scheduling him for chemo even though those treatments historically don't work on thyroid cancer.

"Well," I cautiously continued, "I'm excited to find out the gender of the babies in June. If one of them is a boy, he will have 'Roger' as his middle name."

He smiled when I told him that. Looking back, those were telling smiles. I don't think my dad thought he was going to make it, but he was just fighting the fight for us.

By April, my father had a tracheotomy and a feeding tube but was still trying to be strong and manly. When we all looked at him, that character is what we saw and will always see. My father was a tall man with broad shoulders and a commanding presence, but he is and forever will be one of the gentlest, kindest, and most accepting people I will ever know. He was my very first best friend, and I didn't want to let go.

# Chapter 14

# HEIDI

The good news for Susan didn't stop at multiples. With the start of my doctor visits in April, we learned that the due date would be Halloween of 2008, on her favorite holiday! I had never been to one of her parties, but I've seen pictures of the fifty-plus attendants at her revelry, and it's evident that she is the go-to girl for anything to do with Halloween!

Soon, I met up with the doctor that proved I didn't have any fibroids. The doctor is a very gentle man and said that he would classify my pregnancy as high risk because of my age—I had already turned forty the previous year, but having multiples was another risk factor.

There was another reason I was appreciative to have had the access to all the in-depth monitoring so early on in this pregnancy; I would have not understood why I was getting so big so fast. By the time I was barely in the third month, I needed to wear maternity uniforms to work because I could not get away with wearing my regular uniform, which consisted of blouses and slacks. Even the attempts to cover myself up with a cardigan were of no use. When I looked down, there was a clearly visible bump about half the size of a beach ball already.

"Wow, Heidi. You're getting so big! How's the baby?" asked a coworker one day when I unsuccessfully tried buttoning up a sweater over my ever-growing belly. Having not really mentioned my plans with coworkers, I realized I must quickly decide if I'd let anyone in on the fact I was carrying babies for another couple.

*How will they take it?* I fretted. Would people hold me in a different regard? Would this person disagree with the process? The airline industry is erratic in that I could not see the people I work with for weeks, months, or years, or I could see people many times a month.

"They're good," I cautiously replied. "I'm actually having twins for another family."

Her eyes widened. "Like a surrogate?"

"Yes, exactly."

"Wow, you're an angel! I'm thankful I won't be pregnant again, so I can't imagine volunteering. How'd you get into that?"

Pleasantly surprised, I told about Susan's and my journey. Thankfully it was well received by many people. Even though my airline is a large company, it is very much like a huge, tight-knit family. I was retelling our story countless times and receiving such good feedback that it kept me in great spirits, which I hope helped create a good environment for the growing babies. It's said that nothing of the carrier's genetics crosses over the placenta, but I was hoping that at least having so much positive energy was beneficial for them.

"This isn't simply altruistic," I'd tell people. "I'm gaining a lot out of the experience as well!"

I was looking forward to reaping my reward of having an additional income stream, which would allow me to be home more often with my own children and spend some much-needed time with them. Also I had to emphasize the fact that it was more than just myself allowing this event to take place: how there was a big team and it was such a multifaceted event that there were so many people giving their expertise and support, that I was just part of the whole. Without all of that support there was no way this miracle would be able to work out. It was also very evident to me how important it was having as much support as Rusty provided, which I may not have experienced had my initial surrogacy inquisition succeeded for me.

As Susan and I talked on the phone, I couldn't help but feel that during the beginning stages of this pregnancy, Susan and her family were having a hard time with these issues of the heart. On one hand, they had this beautiful new path in their lives to look forward to, but also a heavy heart because her father's health had continued spiraling downward. It seemed like he'd have one step forward to getting well, then some complication would arise, and it'd be ten steps back. I wish I had an opportunity to get to know him better because I only was in his presence that one time at the family dinner when we all met before the first transfer.

Soon after we were making arrangements to have the initial "routine" prenatal sonogram preformed in Orlando, and both Susan and Jeff would be present.

"I guess I get to see your turf this time." Susan laughed. We had known each other for close to a year and a half by this point, but with so much activity, time flew by! They chose to stay at a hotel halfway between our house and the sonogram office.

"Let me get you guys coffee on the way to the appointment," I offered. This was a bigger request than it seemed because Jeff was a diehard Dunkin' Donuts coffee fan and Susan was a Starbucks loyalist. I fondly remembered how the barista knew Susan by name and her order when we went through the drive-thru near her house in Chicago prior to the in-vitro transfers.

"Oh, that's a lot of trouble. Don't worry about it," Jeff said.

"It's not a problem," I insisted. "I'm not playing hostess while you're here like you did with me, so it's the least I could do."

Never having been a coffee drinker myself, all was going great 'til I was in line to get Susan's and realized that I did not understand the language nor was I fluent in Starbucks-speak.

"I just, uh, want a large black coffee—however you call it is fine with me. I'll just take whichever is large," I told the barista, extracting my wallet from my purse. When I looked up, he didn't look amused. I guess that was the fifth time he heard it that morning or it just wasn't a good day. Too happy to care, I smiled back at him and hoped to radiate some of my positivity his way.

*That's okay*, I thought while walking out. *I've got better things on the agenda for today.* "Venti" it is.

❧

"Time! for the big reveal," said the technician. "I believe baby A is a boy."

Susan whooped for joy right beside me.

"And next...just trying to find the next place..."

My heart violently strummed against my chest. It may sound childish of me, but I wanted Susan to have a girl along with a boy, as this was her one chance.

"Baby B is another boy!" shouted the technician. I couldn't help but feel letdown.

Susan was the grownup between the two of us. "Are you kidding me? I'm ecstatic to have two boys! What are you talking about...healthy babies is what I want!"

Once again, I saw the beautiful energy that I'm now accustomed to seeing her share.

In all the unique interactions I was able to experience, I found enjoyment in each. Being short in stature and small-boned, I was getting *huge* fast, carrying twins. It was ordinary to run across at least five to ten different coworkers in a month that I may not have seen in years.

"When are you due?" asked one.

"Halloween."

His eyes bulged like a bullfrog's. "Holy guacamole! And you're that big?"

I could see the gears in his head turning while trying to come up with something nice to say after that. So many people would ask about my due date then would try to hide the "Oh my God, and you're *that* big already!" look by quickly asking, "What are you having?" When I'd answer *two boys*, they almost always forgot to continue hiding their thoughts. "Ooooooohhhh!" (*That explains a lot!* I'm sure they were thinking). I always found it hilarious.

Not so hilarious was all the stooping, lifting, and pushing accompanying my job. As I maneuvered the aisle between all the knees and elbows, I had worked so frequently on the aircrafts that I honestly did not think it'd be much of a difference. I couldn't imagine the day where my stomach would undoubtedly become so big that I wouldn't be able to perform my job. I had to provide my company a form that my ob-gyn signed every month stating I was physically fit to work in a flight attendant capacity, and I anticipated that I would be able to carry that out until my eighth month as allowed by our work rules.

When I mentioned that to my ob-gyn, he abruptly cut in. "Oh, no. I'm not letting you work past six months!"

*Ruh-roh*, I thought. *Time for financial shuffling.* Where there was a will, there was a way. I could have asked Susan and Jeff for help, but by that point, I was no longer in it for just the financial gains. This was an endeavor we'd work out on our end to the best of our abilities.

The list of challenges was growing. Even though I'm normally the biggest chowhound, I found myself eyeing even crostinis and water with concern. My acid reflux was a force to be reckoned with. No matter what I put in my mouth, the result wasn't pleasant for the people around me. After one bad belch, Rusty turned and looked at me in shock.

"'Scuse me," I squeaked.

Just as I was receiving well wishes from all of my co-workers, my husband and I would often have strangers start conversations with us while out and about on the town. He had a good time when they'd ask questions by answering, "I don't know, they're not my babies." Well, the person asking about the pregnancy would stare at us completely tongue-tied after that!

Sometimes I would have fun playing along with a quick response of, "Yeah, they're not mine, either." It can be fun to harmlessly disarm people then let them in on the reality. We never had anyone show displeasure whether they approved of the process or not; we always parted with warm wishes.

There is no way it would have been as easy on me throughout the entire pregnancy if Susan and I did not have mutual trust and respect for each other's roles and lives.

"Susan," I wondered aloud over the phone one day, "Do you have any special requests of me during the pregnancy?"

"Holding my kids—oh yeah, that's done!"

"I mean regarding any diet limitations, or maybe including certain things in my routine, like listening to certain music or refraining from any activities?"

Susan laughed.

"Heidi, I know you've done a great job delivering three great kids, and so I trust you'll do exactly the same and keep my boys' best interest at heart. I really do appreciate all that you're doing for my family."

"You're such a sweetheart for showing me concern," I replied gratefully. "But believe me, I've got the easy part! Raising children is what makes a parent, and you'll have a lifetime of trials and tribulations ahead of you to earn your title."

# Chapter 15

# SUSAN

Jeff always said my relationship with my dad was "fun to witness." We understood each other more than anyone else in the world did, or at least I know he "got" me. Even though I never talked about my inner struggles I had since the hysterectomy or being the one responsible for our inability to create a family, he knew how much that weighed on me. Many years prior, my father told me that he asked Jeff's dad if it bothered him that Jeff wouldn't be having any kids—you know, being his only son, no namesake, and so on. I'll never forget what he told me that Jeff's dad had said. He said, "It would bother me if it wasn't Susan." My dad needed for me to know that, and more importantly, I think *he* needed to hear it too.

Now, my dad would never lie to me, but he would do whatever he needed to in order to make me feel better. I never actually knew if it was a true story or not until after my father died. My confirmation came after Payton and Jordan were born. We were visiting Jeff's parents and sharing a tearful conversation about the death of my father and how much we all missed him. I told Jeff's dad that my father had shared what he said about me way back when, and I couldn't even get the whole sentence out before I burst into tears. Jeff's father did, too, so I knew then he said it and meant it. How happy we all were now that Payton and Jordan were here but so very sad my dad never got to meet them.

The last week of April came another move for my father—the final one. He was to come home for home hospice care because there was nothing more they could do for him. My sister and I collected him from the hospital. He was alert and chipper, so one look at him, and you never would have expected we were nearing the end of the battle. The tracheotomy was the only telling sign of his illness. My mom had the house prepared for his arrival home for the last time.

The following days went quickly, as did my father. Some people visited, but mostly we were to make him comfortable as his body prepared for his last breath. Watching all of it happen in front of your eyes is unimaginable, but my dad was a trooper. He would tell us how it felt to feel as if you were in one world while seeing another in front of you. I was sitting in the living room with him one day, just sharing some time with him. He would stare into space and close his eyes and then open them again.

"It's amazing," he said with a rattling breath.

"What is?" I asked softly. I leaned forward to hear him better.

"Going back and forth." He paused. "Seeing people that passed before me and awakening next to you here."

My father is a person who had one of the closest relationships with God that I have ever known in my lifetime, so I knew in his way he was making arrangements with God for when his soul would leave this earth.

After a week of being in home hospice, it was evident it was going to be more difficult than we thought to take care of him. My dad was six feet two, so it became almost impossible for my mom, sister, and the hospice nurses to help him. My mom found they had a space in a local hospice center, and we planned his move to that facility. It was on May 7. I went to work and my mom and sister assisted in the transfer of my father to the center. Feeling overwhelmed and like I needed to get away, I made an appointment for a manicure after work. My mom and sister had gotten my dad settled and had left for the evening, so my intent was to be there in the morning.

While getting my nails done, Jeff called me.

"Are you coming home?"

It was odd for Jeff to call me during something like this in the first place, but his tone was a giveaway.

"Did my father die?" I asked.

"Yes. Just get home."

Unthinking, nails wet or not, I sprinted to my car and talked to Jeff the whole way home. My father had his plan, all right. He waited until he was in a facility. (I don't think he wanted to die at home and leave that memory for my mother.) He, gentleman that he was, waited until my mom and sister had left and I wasn't there either. The hospice nurses said he went peacefully about ten minutes after my mom and sister had left.

Heidi called shortly after.

"Hi," she murmured. "We heard."

I blinked back tears. Though my dad was with the angels, I had my own here on earth on the other end of the line.

"Rusty and I can come up to the funeral, if you'd like."

I didn't think I could handle mixing the two emotional extremes in my life at the same time, so I graciously declined the offer. We were so connected at this point that they completely understood.

No stopping the train, we refocused after my father's death to the arrival of baby A and baby B. Talking names, we had come up with two unisex names, and on Father's Day weekend, we were heading down to Florida to witness the "family jewels or no family jewels" ultrasound. Payton and Jordan were the names chosen.

Anxiously sitting in the ultrasound room, they readied Heidi and scanned her belly for the evidence. As you now know, there they were: Baby A, it's a boy! Baby B, another boy!

*Holy cow!* The names were set, and by the profile of baby B, we thought it looked a lot like my family's side, so baby B would further be known as Jordan Roger, and Baby A, Payton Lee. (Incidentally Lee is a Bowen family namesake. Jeff and both of his parents, and now Payton, bear the same middle name.) We called our parents and family and friends and told them the news.

"This was just the news I was hoping to tell my father," I whispered to Jeff, trying to suppress the tears that wouldn't stop flowing. "I wanted to say his namesake would be here soon."

❀

Now that we knew the sex, we dove into preparations. My sister painted the room jungle-themed; we bought two cribs, and we loaded up on everything we could possibly need like we were anticipating the apocalypse. But—here's the fun part—we still had baby showers to think about!

"It's so strange to be enjoying all the new stuff when Heidi's doing the work," I told Jeff. "Heidi's the special one."

My sister, Mom, and Aunt Carol threw us our first shower. They hosted it at the very same restaurant that we had told my family about the surrogacy, and where my family had met Heidi and Rusty and their daughter when we began the whole journey together. It was a trying day. I saw my mother's tight lips and glossy eyes, and it was as if she were trying to hold in all the opposing emotions of being excited for two new grandchildren while still grieving for the loss of her life partner.

Although beaming, I felt a strange tug on my stomach that wouldn't let me fully enjoy the moment. During each great gift reveal, I grinned with gratitude even though my stomach fell.

"You look like you could use a martini," said my sister. She put one in my hand and patted my shoulder. "Drink up."

Well, shoot. I couldn't turn that down.

"Your glass is empty. Have another!" said my friend.

Before I knew it, my side of the table had a few glasses lined up along the edge. By the end of the event, I put my hand up in the air to make an announcement.

"Guys, I think I'm drunk at my own baby shower." After my stunned look, I snorted and started giggling. I was at my own baby shower, getting served martini after martini—when have you ever heard a mother say *that* before?

# Chapter 16

# *HEIDI*

I had never imagined that showers could be a taxing chore. By the time we neared October, I had to fall back on the couch and catch my breath after each shower. With each week that passed, it was harder and harder to make sure the boys were getting the nutrients they needed—even the sight of food in commercials was making my stomach roll. As much as I love to eat, I never considered for a moment that would be one of the harder issues I was facing by carrying the twins. Just the act of hoisting myself in and out of the SUV took twice as long!

Another unforeseen consideration was wondering that even though I had been participating in a lot of testing, what if the twins were born with some sort of physical or mental limitation? I understand almost any parent would never for a second let that diminish the care and love they would have for their newborn children, but I still could not help wonder how I could potentially be a party to bringing about life-changing challenges for this family. There is always that risk; Mother Nature gets to call the shots, and it's a matter of a family's character how they coexist with that. I made every attempt to put such thoughts on the back burner because there was no indication that at the moment they'd have to wrangle with such circumstances, it is just another consideration to take into account when sincerely contemplating surrogacy.

During my time off, I felt like a newborn infant myself. Most of the time I slept, and the little energy I was able to consume went toward the twins. Simply moving around for everyday tasks exerted me, so I tried to move as little as possible.

"I feel so bad," I groggily told Rusty when I propped myself up against some pillows to choke some food down. "Like I should be helping around the house."

"It's okay, you're just doing your job!" Rusty said. "Bringing the Bowen boys to the world."

When I did get out, I went to Cayla's school events. Even while full to bursting, I sat near the top of the bleachers for her volleyball game. Watching her smiling and laughing, not to mention serving that volleyball with all her strength, my heart swelled with pride.

"I can't wait until Susan gets to experience these special moments," I told Rusty. "Until both she and Jeff get to experience the joys of family life."

He nodded heartily in agreement. Feeling lucky to have my husband so onboard with the arrangements, I knew I wouldn't change a thing about my family life.

When I thought about our family togetherness, though, my thoughts couldn't help but sometimes stray to Susan's father. Susan's dad, Roger, passed away after such a strong struggle to try to combat the relentless, aggressive cancer. When I had told Cayla, I saw her face visibly fall. We both remembered the pages of that special book he gave her and his warm mannerisms. To this day, I know there are events that reassure Susan that her father's spirit is still with them, and I am sure that they'll take any bit of time they can get with him, even if it is in spirit. He would be watching right alongside Susan and Jeff once their kids were playing in sporting events. We all knew it.

Last day in September.

It was an average day. I tried getting out to run some simple errands with my husband and daughter, but I was so worn out that Cayla took the wheel.

"Just go ahead and drop me off at the hardware store," Rusty said. "You both can wait out here." As Rusty jumped out and went in, I leaned back and closed my eyes. Cayla accelerated and then drove off to find a parking spot. Losing perspective in my sleepiness, I suddenly shot up.

"Hey, you're going to jump that curb!" I warned. My whole body was tensed.

"Don't worry, Momma. I got this." Cayla did, and lo and behold—there was no curb to hit. She was simply parking. Oh boy.

When we came home, a nap was in order. Simply getting into the SUV was enough physical exertion for the whole week, if you asked me. Effortlessly, I fell into a deep sleep.

When I woke up, I tried lifting my body up. I felt like my lower half was anchored, or that I was a beached whale. Even though the date for the C-section was scheduled for October 15 now, I couldn't imagine another couple of weeks. They seemed so ready to pop out!

As if a warning, I stood up, and my water broke. You guys know what happens next.

Rusty and Cayla each put an arm around me and led me to the car. Not sure where the energy came from—and you can call me a control freak if you want to—but I wanted to drive, so I was the one who drove us all to the hospital! Being high-risk and having already had a scheduled C-section, there was no waiting around once I was admitted into the hospital.

"Cayla, I think you're the reason they came early," I teased. "You scared them out by almost jumping that curb, even if there wasn't one in that parking lot!"

To the front of the line to next available operation room, and it was show time for baby A and baby B. My husband and daughter were with me all throughout the prep for the C-section. Early on in the pregnancy, Rusty made a point to make sure Susan knew we both wanted her to be the one person that was allowed into the operating room because Rusty felt she deserved to enjoy the full experience, and I of course agreed with that notion. Seeing how she was unable to make it in time, my husband did come into the operating room and took as many pictures as he could to preserve the boys' first moments for their parents. As soon as they both were delivered and on their way to the NICU, Rusty and Cayla called Susan and Jeff.

"They're here! It's their birthday!" Susan said. Cayla and Rusty then proceeded to sing "Happy Birthday to the Bowen Boys" into the phone.

"I also have about a hundred photos of the delivery," Rusty said. "I'll forward them to you guys ASAP!"

"Thank you so, so much," Susan said. "We cannot wait!"

What an eventful day. Normal procedures were to have the Bowen boys spend time in the neonatal intensive care unit for a short observation because they were delivered from a pregnancy classified as high risk. However, thankfully they were both very healthy and were quickly moved to the floor where I had a room.

Looking down at the sleeping cherubs, I saw their pudgy cheeks and swathes of blond hair.

"They look as healthy as can be," Rusty remarked. Even arriving a full month early, Payton was born at five pounds and fourteen ounces, and Jordan was at five pounds and ten ounces. Susan and Jeff made some tough little guys. I just couldn't wait for them to meet their handiwork in the flesh.

# Chapter 17

# SUSAN

As I was driving back from work on September 30, 2008, Rusty called me.

"Hello, Susan! We've taken Heidi to the hospital, and it's the real deal!"

I almost slammed on the brakes in the middle of the highway. My surroundings were now a blur.

"What? Oh my God! Thank you for telling me—oh my God! I'm calling Jeff to book tickets right now!"

As soon as I hung up, I shrieked. I couldn't believe it! But there was no time to dwell on it; we had to get our butts down to Florida! I punched speed dial to let Jeff know the news.

"Jeff, tell the airlines to schedule our flight. Let's choose first class so we have space for the boys when we bring them home—ahh, can you believe it!?"

We weren't going to make it for the actual delivery, but we used our points to do just that. They were born on September 30, 2008, at exactly 10:22 PM. We would be meeting them for the first time the following day.

Farley greeted me at the door once I was home, excited as if he already knew the news. He pawed me with his big, clumsy hands and was all tail as it wagged and nearly knocked the flower vase over.

"Your brothers are here!" I announced, rambunctiously turning him over on the floor and rubbing his belly. "We're putting you in doggy day care so we can go get 'em!"

Thankfully, Jeff's parents lived in Florida, so they were to meet us at the airport with the baby carriers we had shipped down and drive us to the hospital. It was all so surreal that the most I can say is that we made a mad dash to Florida.

Fast forward to the elevator. Jeff and I squeezed hands. The beep signifying we were up another floor seemed to mock me—it was gruelingly slow! Once we were on the maternity floor, we bolted out of the elevator, powerwalking through the hall. As we rounded the corner to Heidi's room, my heart was trying to rip itself out of my chest. But then Heidi's room—oh my God, Heidi's room…

There she was, one baby in her arm and the other cradled in Rusty's. The moment was inexplicable. My eyes moved toward Heidi's, which were sparkling with joy. Right there, I wept.

"Come meet your son," she said. She gently placed Jordan in my arms, and Rusty gave Jeff Payton. We were actually holding our biological children that Heidi delivered to us.

When we were able to move our transfixed eyes from our new bundles of joy, we saw Jeff's parents' eyes welling with tears.

"Pictures!" I said.

I knew my mom would especially love to see this sight. Forwarding them back to my family at home and updating friends on everything that was going on, I felt like the happiest woman alive. Once that was done, we sat and stared at their beautiful faces, marveling at the gift.

Previously, I had always been too nervous to hold a newborn and admittedly avoided it when possible. But when holding my own children for the first time, that feeling just vanished. They looked up at me with big doe eyes and babbled adorably. We fed them their formula and waited for dirty diapers to come so we could practice our skills. Nurses and doctors would come and check on all of us, and when visiting hours would end, we would say good night to them both and head back to our housing. I rested the palms of my hands on their silky, chunky arms and didn't want to part from them. It was so surreal. We were simply overwhelmed.

We were to take them home on a plane a mere three days after they were born, and we had a doctor's note and all necessary paperwork. Normally babies that small are not allowed to fly, and for a moment, we thought we'd need to wait longer, as Jordan's bilirubin levels were high. They put the special light in his bassinet for twenty-four hours, and lo and behold, we were cleared to take them home.

Those three days were a blur—lots of laughs, photos, and love. When I gathered stray jackets, water bottles, books, and blankets from the hospital room, I felt the familiar constriction of my throat indicating an impending emotional moment.

*What on earth could I say to Heidi?* I wondered. Can you imagine? Over a year of prep and almost thirty-five weeks and four days of carrying our children, and I was at a loss for words. When I turned around and saw Heidi's smiling face, I lost it and threw myself into her arms for a hug.

"Heidi, I love you," I said. "Thank you. Thank you so much."

As we pulled away, she looked deeply into my eyes. "You're welcome."

She sounded like an angel. She *is* an angel.

"Be careful putting them in the carrier," Jeff told me.

Admittedly not being a real "baby person" up until that point, I had no idea the attention a newborn baby can attract, let alone two three-day-old newborns going through security at an airport. Also adding a level of confusion, there I was in my slender frame with two babies in my arms, and people were doing double takes.

"You mean you gave birth three days ago?" asked one woman as we waited to board.

Jeff and I joked, "Yeah, there we were walking around Disney, and her water broke, out popped the twins, and now we are heading home."

How do you even begin to tell the story of what just happened to complete strangers? We played around with our responses.

Later we boarded the plane like rock stars. They called first-class passengers, and the flight attendants took special care escorting us to our seats once they saw what we had with us. As others boarded the plane behind us and scurried to their seats, we truly felt like celebrities. We told our story to many within earshot, and one woman wanted to take our picture to send off to her daughter, marveling at our story and at the two precious and perfect passengers we had on our laps.

They were so quiet the whole way back that I found myself checking to make sure they were still breathing. Of course they were—their tiny little chests rising and falling gently with each peaceful breath. I never knew how much I could worry until I became a mother.

"Take this bottle," I cooed. "You won't feel ear pressure that way."

I must have stared at Jordan the whole flight.

Once we landed, I called my sister who was our ride home along with my mom. As we headed into the baggage claim terminal, I saw my mother running toward us, camera in hand and tears in her eyes.

"Oh my God! Oh my God, they are beautiful!" She looked to the heavens and said, "Honey, they are here!" Then she wept.

We gathered our luggage and found my sister in her van at arrivals, bouncing up and down to see Payton and Jordan. She saw us coming toward her and started crying.

"They are beautiful!" she said. We hurried into the van, and she drove us home. Again, I couldn't keep my eyes off of their precious faces. They were here; they were ours. Had I really known happiness prior to that moment? Looking down at their round, rosy faces, I knew we were ushering in a grand chapter of life and a whole new world of possibilities.

*Thank you, God. Thank you, Heidi.*

# *Epilogue*

That December, Heidi and her daughter came to visit. The boys were napping in their cribs, still small as baby dolls but pleasantly plump and serene as I'd ever seen them.

"I can't get over how big and healthy they look," Heidi said.

"They're our little chunks," I said affectionately, brushing the back of my index finger against Payton's silky cheek. "You, on the other hand, look just like you did before the pregnancy."

It was true; Heidi was small and dainty once again.

"Well, thank you. I feel different, though."

"How so?"

"I miss the boys, but not so much them personally as much as the experience. You go from people asking you on an almost daily basis about your pregnancy and being able to explain to people the miracle you are providing someone in their lives, to just being a 'regular person' again."

"I know exactly what you mean. I was a regular person and became a mother instantly," I replied. I remembered the sleepless nights and adjusting to motherhood—and those three months off for maternity leave when I hadn't even been pregnant? It felt so random. Well, I wasn't going to complain.

"I hope you're telling people you gave birth but instantly got back into shape," Heidi joked.

"Ha. Why not!"

As the boys grew and became more expressive, it became that much more obvious that Jordan had a little piece of my dad's soul in him. I catch him looking up at me in such a dad-like manner, and so have my mom and sister. It's comforting, even if we were looking for it, but even Jeff would say from time to time how uncanny it was. I feel my dad around all the time but miss him terribly. Although I know he can see me being a mother now, I wish I could have shared it with him here on earth.

Jeff was in charge of morning duty, whether dropping the boys off at my sister's or waiting home for the babysitter to arrive. I was in charge of pick up and afternoon duties. Racing home from work, all I wanted to do was see their smiling faces. The first few weeks back to work were hard. Like any new mother who returns to work after a maternity leave, it is bittersweet. My sister was fantastic; she sent me pictures from her phone or posted them to Facebook during the day for me to see. The days just flew by and they still do: rush to get the boys, rush home to plop them in a stroller, and walk the ever-growing Farley (he's now 170 pounds, by the way).

We felt like minor celebrities in our circle of friends. Everyone would ask us if it was okay that they told people our story. The general public seemed unaware that something like this could be so successful and go as well as it did. We loved telling the story, but to this day, we still get the open jaw and reactions of disbelief from some outsiders. Having not lived through it ourselves, I think our natural reaction would have been somewhat the same. It's just hard to wrap your head and emotions around. Many people don't even know what to say when I just mention casually that we used a surrogate to have our children. They don't seem to hear the whole statement and keep talking before suddenly stopping. Then the onslaught of questions:

"Wait, what did you say?"

"Oh my gosh! How did that work?"

"Do you still talk to Heidi?"

"Was it hard for her to give them up?"

"Why did you use a surrogate?"

"How did you trust that she would do everything 'right?'"

In the first year of their lives, we answered those questions time and time again as our close friends and relatives each were touched by meeting and being a part of Payton's and Jordan's lives. Constantly we send pictures and keep in close touch with Heidi and Rusty. Our natural inclination was even to invite them to their first birthday party.

Heidi had admitted to us in the past that large social crowds weren't exactly her "thing." The boys' first birthday party was going to involve at least fifty people, but they accepted the invitation. As I spread the word to my friends and family that they would be in attendance, people were jumping out of their skin to meet our angel.

One of my best friends said, "Oh my gosh, I have so many questions for her! I can't wait to corner her and talk to her about everything!"

To that, one of my other best friends responded, "Susan just told you Heidi doesn't exactly love social events, so give her some breathing room, would ya?"

We had a hell of a party for the boys—so many people celebrating their first year of life and how they arrived in our arms. Again, it was bittersweet. My mom, sister, and I had our moments of missing our father. Boy, would he have loved this celebration and to be here in the flesh. We felt his presence, of course, but many in the room also knew him well, and occasionally, we'd hear people reflect on that.

The party drew to an end, and Heidi's premiere introduction to everyone was extraordinary. Later on, she told me how many people came up to her to thank her for the gift she had given not only Jeff and I, but to everyone that we knew. She truly had a remarkable effect on everyone there and continues to do so as our story literally lives on.

Today, whenever I look at the children and Heidi in the same room, I feel I'll burst with gratitude and love. Those three people in my life are some of the best people to walk into it. Heidi and I now have an inexplicable bond; she is my friend, my confidant, and my sister in this journey of life.

I often said I'm sure I would have been able to live my life without children; many people do and do so happily. But because of Heidi's generosity, I have opened the door to a new facet of life, learning, and love that I never would have been able to experience. I am truly grateful; it is something I will never be able to repay. The Sunday before Mother's Day each year, our family has coined "Surrogate Mother's Day" and we MacGyver a card to look something of the sort and send off a special gift to Heidi. You see, without her I never could have been a mother, so she gets recognized before me.

Families are built in many ways and include many types of people. Ours not only includes Payton and Jordan now, but also Heidi's entire family who supported her and me throughout this journey. We love them as if they were our own blood.

—Susan

They all went back to Chicago when the boys were three days old, and we stayed on in Orlando. I can say that I never once felt like I was giving up any child because I didn't. It was completely reconciled in my heart prior to the onset of our experience together that these children are, were, and always will be Susan and Jeff's babies. Biologically they are from both their own lineage. Science and society have come so far since the first test tube baby was born in 1979, but it's somewhat still of a mystery to so many. I knew that there was something in my heart that would allow me to carry this out and see it through without feelings of attachments that make it such a taboo subject.

Something that has helped me feel confident throughout the entire process with Susan and Jeff was the fact that they had been open to having Rusty and me be a part of their boys' lives in whatever capacity that we all felt comfortable with. After all that we had gone through together, we were aware enough to know that. We are family now. Knowing that I was welcomed to watch the boys grow helped me feel reassured and validated all the energy that we all gave to this miracle journey, making the parting acceptable.

Susan and I never intended for our surrogacy memoir to be a "how to" guide because we aren't experts in the medical field, and as you probably have figured out by now, even the best-laid plans can have roadblocks and diversions. The laws regarding such procedures are vast and ever-changing. It's not our intent to disseminate exact steps on how to make it work for you. We can just offer hope through retelling our trials and tribulations, and if that helps even one person through any personal trial, then we've done another good thing.

We also have both come to the conclusion that the voice I so clearly heard while watching the video back in 2009 suggesting this book be written was that of her father. Perhaps he was just putting it out there that he was proud of his growing family and wanted to spread the word.

Thanks, Roger. What a blessing to be an integral part of someone else's blessing!